LETTERS FROM
MEDJUGORJE

LETTERS FROM MEDJUGORJE

WAYNE WEIBLE

PARACLETE PRESS
Orleans, Massachusetts

Passages in italics throughout the book are from the messages
received by the visionaries of Medjugorje.

All Scripture passages are from the New American Bible.

1st Printing,   June 1991

ISBN: 1-55725-021-9
Printed in the United States of America

Dedicated to my children
who have opened their hearts
and listened —
Angela, Kennedy, Lisa, Michael, Rebecca
and Steven

. . . And with special love
to Courtney,
a courageous little friend

Acknowledgements

This book would be incomplete without grateful acknowledgement of the support and assistance from family, friends, and fellow pilgrims of Medjugorje. My humble thanks to —

my wife, Terri, as always a full partner in the mission that has been given to us, and an excellent unpaid editor and proof-reader;

Maureen Murphy, my hard-working secretary, who keeps track of where I've been, where I'm going—and everything in between; and Christina Wyatt, who has to open and sort all of the letters received;

Maria Cartwright for arranging my travel and helping me out of numerous binds created by changed schedules;

Caritas of Birmingham, for the compilation of messages in Words From Heaven, and also Dave Golub's Live The Messages;

David Manuel, invaluable as teacher, editor, collaborator, and friend;

and all of you who took the time to write your stories through letters which inspired this book.

Foreword

Medjugorje—The first account I had from someone who had actually been there was in 1985, from David du Plessis. Called the "Father of Modern Pentecost," David was more instrumental than anyone else in the wildfire spread of the Charismatic Movement (which swept me into the Kingdom in 1970). *Time* called him one of the spiritual giants of our age—and so did John Paul II. It was my privilege to be the collaborator on his last book before he died, *Simple & Profound.*

In the final chapter of that book, he described his trip to the little mountain village in central Yugoslavia, where God was doing something extraordinary. David was fourscore years then, but his spiritual discernment and acumen were as sharp as ever. He went with the blessing and encouragement of his friend, Cardinal Kuharic of Yugoslavia.

He also went as a "fruit inspector"—for as Jesus had taught His disciples: "A good tree cannot bring forth evil fruit, neither can a corrupt tree bring forth good fruit." [Matt. 7:18] In his long, distinguished career in the Lord's service, David had steered Pentecostals worldwide and Charismatics of all denominations through many dangerous waters. Was Medjugorje the ultimate deception of the Angel of Light at the end of this age? If anyone could discern "the fine Italian hand of the devil," it would be David.

"I did not see Mary," he told me. "But what I did see convinced me that this is of God. I saw revival—on a scale I'd given up hope of ever seeing again in my lifetime. And," he smiled, "I did not find one piece of bad fruit."

He urged me to go and see for myself, but I was too busy. Two years later, my wife went, and the fruit of Medjugorje in her life was undeniable. Barbara had made a total commitment to Christ many years before, but over there her relationship with Him so deepened that she— and our life together—would never be the same.

Before Medjugorje, for instance, she had been a crossword puzzle devotee; anyone disturbing her before she finished the morning puzzle risked a cross word or two themselves. Now she forsook the puzzle, making that her morning quiet time with God, which she protected as a lioness would her cubs.

I waited for Medjugorje to wear off, but it never did. It went deeper. Gradually my wife put God's will above all else—to the point where nothing else even mattered. For seventeen years and sixteen books I had been professing to do the same. But next to her, I could see how shallow my own faith was.

So in the spring of 1988, when she urged me to offer to help Wayne Weible with his first book, I was willing to hear the still, small voice of God's Spirit confirm that this was of Him. Nonetheless, when Wayne came to speak at our community, I listened intently for anything the least bit off-center spiritually. Had there been the slightest blip on the screen—

But there were no blips. Laced with self-deprecating humor, Wayne's testimony was honest to the point of transparency—and anointed. Mary had called him to spread the message of Medjugorje as far and wide as possible, and to the best of his ability he was being obedient to his call.

Was I?

We met and prayed together, and three weeks later were on our way to Medjugorje. I went open-hearted, but wishing that God had used someone other than Mary. Seventeen years before, I had been the original editor of Logos, the first Charismatic publishing house, and had absorbed all the anti-Mary bias of centuries of Protestantism and decades of Pentecostalism. Well, I would soon see for myself.

What I found was what my friend, David du Plessis, had found: a countryside transformed. A church filled with local inhabitants, praying and singing from the heart—in the middle of the week, at the end of a long working day. I, too, had the heart-wrenching experience of having an ancient, black-clad woman insist that I change places with her. I was to sit in the pew, while she knelt on the stone floor. No one can go through that without being broken.

In Marija's home where we stayed, a door which was always closed was once left ajar. I glanced in. On the floor were four made-up mattresses—so that Wayne and I could sleep in beds.

There were countless other instances of anonymous and/or spontaneous acts of love. For many in that village, loving one's neighbor as oneself had become instinctive.

And yet—in my own heart something was still lacking. On our last day there, alone in the grove behind the church, I lay on my back under the cedars. Gazing up at the sky, I asked God why the thing which had happened to my wife here, had not happened to me.

I noted that some clouds had formed a perfect cross. As I watched them pass over me, His answer seemed to form in my heart: *Barbara was converted here. You were converted on Cape Cod, seventeen years ago.*

Then, Father, what do You want of me?

You already know: Surrender.

Three years have passed since then. People say I've changed. But all I can see are the places I haven't surrendered. And they are ever before me.

To my Protestant brethren I would say: approach Medjugorje with an open heart. God is doing something there so crucial that we cannot afford to miss it. It is not just for Catholics; it is for all mankind. He does not care by what denomination we call ourselves. He cares for our hearts—do they yearn for His?

If we are at the foot of His Cross, looking up at Him, they do; they cannot help it.

And all who kneel there, whatever they are called, are truly one.

—David Manuel

Introduction

Dear Wayne,
    Medjugorje has made me aware of the reality of
God in such a way that I now want to devote my
life to Him. I don't know yet what He wants me to
do, but I'm searching and trying to let Him guide
me. I haven't been the same since going to
Medjugorje and I want to return. I just had to
write and tell you what happened to me while I
was there. . .

Thus begins one of literally thousands of letters I have received from people who have been touched by Medjugorje and the messages of the Blessed Virgin Mary. They are words of testimony of the magnificent fruits derived in ten years of Her daily apparitions there, ranging from short notes to mini-manuscripts. They tell of miraculous changes in lives.

Frankly, this is not the next book I planned to write. But in December, 1990, something happened that caused me to change horses in mid-stream.

On an interstate just outside of St. Louis, I was in the back seat of an automobile, working with a laptop computer to answer letters; it was my intent during this long, two-hour drive between speaking engagements to also work on the outline of my next book. I planned it to be the companion to the first, picking up where the other left off.

Suddenly while reading a particularly touching letter, I looked up and said to my hosts in the front seat, "You know, I need to do a book on the letters I get from people; it's been on my mind for a long time and just now, I felt that Our Lady was saying to me: *'do it!'* "

I stopped working on the other book and immediately began this one. After all, that's what the Holy Messenger of Medjugorje was asking of me—and by now, I was getting used to listening to her—and doing what she asked!

This holy messenger, who is the handmaid of the Father, spouse of the Holy Spirit, and loving mother of the Son, comes to teach us wisdom and love. And those who have heard the oft-repeated requests for prayer, fasting and penance, during her ten years of appearances at Medjugorje, feel an exhilarating desire to share them with others.

A common thread among the new converts to the gospel of Jesus Christ—the foundation for Mary's messages—is a sudden and often startling personal conversion to the ways of God. It is a path many converts have never taken, or have forgotten. Often, it is accompanied by an inexplicable sense of individual peace.

There are many books on the events of Medjugorje. Most attempt to give a full, detailed accounting or explanation—or both—of the visits of the Virgin Mary to this tiny village located in the mountains of central Yugoslavia. That was the goal of my first book.

This book is different; it attempts to share the personal, sometimes intimate feelings and opinions of those who learned of the apparitions, and then reacted to its basic message of return to God. Most of them are positive; a few aren't. Some are sad and filled with despair, and others cannot accept that God would renew His Word, His New

Covenant with us through His mother.

Not everyone who hears about Medjugorje believes it is authentic and is immediately converted. There is no spiritual magic taking place in this little village with the unpronounceable name; acceptance or rejection of its fruits still depends on the free-will of the individual.

Interspersed among the letters are stories and experiences gleaned from my years of traveling the world to bring the message to others. There is also a scattering of personal reflections on different parts of the messages, as well as many of the actual messages from the Blessed Virgin Mary as given to the young visionaries during the first ten years of the apparitions. These, I feel, are the most important part of the book.

The final ingredient is related Scripture texts to further explain what is happening in Medjugorje.

Most of the letters and stories have been edited and condensed in order to include as many as possible. In a majority of the letters, names have been changed to protect the confidentiality of the writer. Last names are rarely used for the same reason. I have tried to preserve them just as they were sent to me. For that reason, personal composition and style are basically unchanged.

The preeminent purpose for "Letters From Medjugorje" is to allow readers to identify with other ordinary people like themselves who have experienced the love and peace of the renewed Gospel messages. It is for both those familiar with the apparitions, and those who are reading about them for the first time.

As of this writing, Mary continues to come to Medjugorje to visit daily with four of the original six young visionaries. The visits are much briefer now. But they continue to occur. That of itself, is a sign of the love of God for all of his children.

The village and its people have changed; they have

suffered the growing pains of fame and fortune-seekers—those who would profit from God's phenomenal gift to us. Our Lady says of this that those who take from the pilgrims will be judged on their deeds, and those from whom they have taken, will be blessed.

Despite inevitable commercialism, it continues to draw hungry souls from around the world. The experience of Medjugorje is the same today for the first-time pilgrim, as it was for those of us who came in earlier years. It is on- going spiritual grace.

And for that reason, the letters will continue to come.

There are still many other things that Jesus did, yet if they were written about in detail, I doubt there would be room enough in the entire world to hold the books to record them. [John 21:25]

1

"God Exists and He loves you..."

"Dear children, I invite everyone to start living in God's love. . . I am your mother and therefore, I want to lead you all to perfect holiness. I want everyone of you to be happy here on earth and everyone of you to be with me in heaven.

This is, dear children, the reason of my coming here and my desire. Thank you for responding to my call."—May 25, 1987

The first invitation came on June 24, 1981; six teenage youths in the little rural village of Medjugorje, Yugoslavia, reported that the Virgin Mary, mother of Jesus Christ, had appeared to them on a nearby hillside. According to these young people, she has been returning every day since, with messages for the whole world, similar to the one above.

It began in a quiet, simple way—a way very much in keeping with daily life in the sleepy little village located in the mountains of central Yugoslavia. Two teenage Croatian girls, having finished their chores for the day, went out for a casual evening stroll.

Ivanka Ivankovic, 16, and her friend from the northern city of Sarajevo, Mirjana Dragicevic, 15, wanted to get away from family and friends for awhile on this warm June evening. Mirjana always came to Medjugorje to visit her grandmother in the summers and had become Ivanka's best friend. The two left a note at the home of a third close companion, Vicka Ivankovic, 17, asking her to join them when she awoke from an afternoon nap. The three girls were nearly inseparable, spending most of their time away from daily chores together.

On this particular evening, they had another motive to be alone; Mirjana had brought her portable radio so that they could listen to music, share girl-talk—and smoke cigarettes away from the disapproving eyes of family. It was a small, mischievous ritual performed by the trio on past occasions.

Vicka, exhausted from taking school exams that morning, still had not arrived as the two began to make their way home around 6:30. Lost in personal thought and trailing her friend by a few yards, Ivanka casually glanced to her right and was startled to see a brilliant flash of light half-way up the rocky, thistle-covered hill that overlooked their village. In the center of the strange light was the unmistakable silhouette of a young woman, holding an infant.

"Mirjana! Mirjana!" she stammered, unsure and frightened by what she was seeing, "look, look up the hill, it's — *Gospa!*"

Her city-bred friend, wary of the practical jokes of her best friend, continued to stare straight ahead. With a wry smile she sarcastically replied, "Come on, Ivanka, who are you kidding—why would Our Lady come to us? We're nobody!" She kept walking toward the row of cinderblock houses lining the road ahead.

The young Croatian teenager, certain from her Catholic upbringing that this was indeed "Gospa"—the Blessed Virgin Mary—was uncertain whether to remain there or go after Mirjana to convince her this was not a joke. She feared the beautiful woman in the light would disappear if she left. Finally, she sprinted after Mirjana, catching up with her as she stopped to speak to a young 13-year-old girl of her acquaintance, on her way to bring the family's sheep home.

"Mirjana, I *did* see Gospa, *I really did!*" she insisted, imploring her to return with her to see if the figure was still there. "Come on, Milka," she said to the young girl, "you come with us, too!"

They rushed back to the spot; the figure was still there. As they stared in fascination and fear, Vicka shouted to them from down the road. She had finally come to join her companions. "Hurry, Vicka, we see Gospa!" Mirjana yelled to her, pointing excitedly to the side of the hill.

Vicka, thinking they were seeing snakes, and shocked they would joke about seeing Gospa, quickly ran in the opposite direction. She came upon two boys she knew well, both named Ivan, who as they would later admit, were helping themselves to apples in trees belonging to one of their neighbors. She convinced them that Mirjana and Ivanka were trying to scare her; or, that they truly saw something unusual up on the hill. The three of them hurried back to the original place of the sighting and instantly saw the same image as the others.

Frightened, Ivan Dragicevic, the younger of the two Ivans, ran away to his home which was close by; the other young people stayed, some praying, some crying quietly, all of them now quite sure of what they were seeing. Even though they lived under the oppression of an atheistic, Communist government, there was a strong Catholic faith in God ingrained in the community, despite the harassment of local government and the mandatory school classes on atheism.

These young people *knew* they were seeing the Blessed

Virgin Mary. Such unwavering faith would serve them well in the days ahead.

Time seemed to stand still as they stared at the beautiful young woman tenderly cradling an infant. She gently beckoned to them with her other hand to come up the side of the hill to where she was standing. Extremely frightened, the children did not move.

As darkness descended, a light mist began to fall. One by one, the youths reluctantly drifted home, excitedly telling family members about what they had seen. Parents, frightened and suspicious, firmly ordered the young people not to tell others. They feared added harassment by local police or ridicule by neighbors. Nevertheless, the story of the event spread through the little village like wildfire. The seed of the most powerful religious phenomenon of our time had been planted.

Little did these young people realize that soon most of them would be caught up in an ongoing miracle that would forever alter their lives—as well as those of their neighbors in tiny Medjugorje.

The next day at approximately the same time, four of the original young people felt an inexplicable urge to return to the spot where they had first witnessed the image. The older of the Ivans, 22, thought such things were for children and ignored the inner call; Milka Pavlovic, whose mother had taken her to distant fields to work, was not able to leave. But Milka's sister Marija, 17, and her 10-year-old cousin, Jakov Colo, who was at the Pavlovic home when the others came by to get her, went with them.

By this small twist of fate Marija and Jakov would join Ivanka, Mirjana, Vicka and Ivan, as the six young Croatians who would become world-famous visionaries in the longest continuing series of daily apparitions of the Virgin Mary ever recorded.

The youths assembled on the road in the exact spot

where they had witnessed the apparition the day before. This time they were accompanied by a small band of about eighty villagers; word had spread that Gospa might have visited their community.

Again, on this second day the beautiful young woman appeared in a flash of light, alone this time. When she beckoned for them to come up the hill to where she was standing, they literally flew up the side of the hill at a rate of speed that normally would be humanly impossible.

The startled group of curious villagers, able to see the flash of light but not the image of the woman, raced down the road to the pathway leading to the top of the hill. As they arrived panting and gasping for breath, they found the six youngsters huddled together on their knees. Each of them was staring fixedly, slightly upward at the same spot, their mouths moving as if in conversation, yet nothing could be heard or seen by the villagers. The children seemed to be in a trance.

The six youths would later relate what had happened during the approximately 15 minutes the image reportedly appeared to them. They felt as if they were out of normal time and space and saw only the beautiful woman bathed in the unusual light; after a few moments of recovery, they began to ask a steady stream of questions:

"Who are you?"

"I am the Blessed Virgin Mary, mother of Jesus."

"Why have you come?"

"I have come because there are many devout believers here. I want to be with you to convert and reconcile everyone to my Son, Jesus. . . I have come to tell you that God exists, and that He loves you!"

"What do you want of the people?"

"I want those who do not see me to believe as firmly as you do!"

And finally they asked the question that somewhere in

our spiritual growth, each of us asks: "Why did you choose us?"

She smiled at them, paused, and then said, *"My dear little ones, I do not always choose the best people!"*

How well these teenagers—two who had quietly stolen away to smoke forbidden cigarettes, and two others who were blatantly helping themselves to a neighbor's apples — understood this particular answer!

I was soon to personally appreciate the irony of what she had said. As a Lutheran Protestant and a journalist by profession, my faith was lukewarm at best. My interest in first learning of the apparitions taking place in Medjugorje was simply to write one story for the four weekly newspapers my wife, Terri and I owned and operated. Ten years earlier, I had gone through a traumatic divorce after fourteen years of a marriage that produced four children. Out of anger over that divorce, I had walked away from all churches for more than seven years. No, I was definitely "not the best people."

In October, 1985, I first learned of what was going on in the little village, from a casual discussion of modern-day miracles during a Sunday school class. Wanting to know more for my newspaper column, I was able to obtain a small book and a video made approximately four years after the beginning of the daily apparitions. The case was impressive, because six isolated, uneducated youths were involved; it would be difficult for them to maintain a hoax for such a long period of time.

In true journalistic fashion, I was untouched spiritually. My training was to look first for facts, to see or touch or in some way verify events—*to be objective!* This so-called supernatural spiritual phenomenon was no exception.

A few evenings later Terri and I decided to watch the video—me to gain additional research material for the article, and her out of mild curiosity.

As the video played, I found myself shaking my head and murmuring over and over, "This is incredible!" I immediately believed it was authentic. The last bit of journalistic objectivity drained away as the camera observed the visionaries up close just before the start of an apparition. The young Croatians, now four years older, began to pray. Simultaneously, in mid-sentence, they stopped and fell to their knees. All were staring at the same spot, oblivious to the crowd pressing around them or the flash cameras going off in their faces.

Suddenly, I felt a strange sensation. Someone—or something—was speaking to me. But it was not an audible voice; the words forming within me were gentle and soft: *"You are my son, and I am asking you to do my Son's will. . ."*

I went numb. This was real! The Blessed Virgin Mary was speaking to me! This was impossible! But it was happening.

"Oh no, God! Not me!" I murmured. "You couldn't possibly be asking me!"

The message continued: *"I am asking you to write about the events of Medjugorje, to give up your present work and to make the spreading of these messages your life mission."*

Though I knew it was the Virgin Mary giving the message, my response was to God. I don't know why; it just was. I felt totally unworthy. Because of my past life, I would ask a thousand times over: "Why me?"

My acceptance was not a bold "yes," but a hesitant, frightened "I'll try."

In the next four years, personal confirmation of what I was being asked to do was revealed to me in many ways. In the beginning, one article quickly became a series of four and ultimately four more. These were published in tabloid form, and as of this writing some 27 million copies have been distributed throughout the world. Our businesses were sold in April, 1986, and the following month I made my first trip to Medjugorje. Before the year was out, newspapering has been replaced with a full itinerary of lecturing tours on Medjugorje.

My "yes" was not immediate. It would take hours of prayer, months of reading Scripture, and several years of on-the-job learning to respond to the basic messages she had come to give.

The messages she gives to the world through the visionaries at Medjugorje, ask us to pray unceasingly with the heart, to fast at least one day a week on bread and water, and to do penance for those who are our neighbors. In essence, they are a synopsis of Jesus' Gospel message. Prayer, fasting, and penance—these are the foundation stones of the messages. Incorporating them into our daily lives leads first to repentance and reconciliation, and eventually to ongoing conversion. These embody the message of Medjugorje.

From the beginning, the young visionaries of Medjugorje responded with a yes. After undergoing weeks of harassment and questioning from local Communist authorities who felt threatened by the throngs now filling the little hamlet, they received the same treatment from their own priests and neighbors as well. Under this duress, they faithfully stuck to their testimony.

Strong, confirming evidence of their stories can be found in ten years of God's grace that has flowed from the little village. More than 20 million people have journeyed to Medjugorje to witness and experience for themselves the presence of heaven on earth. And their lives have touched many times that number. Dozens of books, video and audio tapes feed the insatiable spiritual hunger so many have to find God and truly become His children.

The visionaries, priests, and villagers have been probed, investigated, and questioned by top theology experts of the Catholic Church and others. Experts in medicine and science have done the same. None of them can prove the apparitions are authentic; but neither have they been able to prove they are not. The tests and investigations do, however, confirm that something physiologically extraordinary is happening when the visionaries go into a state of ecstasy.

For those who have experienced spiritual conversion through the events of Medjugorje, the first message given by Mary to the six youths on that second day gives reason enough to believe: *"I have come to tell you that God exists. . . and that He loves you!"*

The appearance of the woman holding the infant Jesus in her arms on that first day gives us a beautiful image to accompany her answer. She stood there overlooking a village that very much resembles Bethlehem. It was as if she had come to rebirth Jesus—to renew the Gospel of the Savior of the world in a time of urgent need.

It is that image—of people discovering the love of Jesus and Mary—that spurs them to take pen in hand and write letters from Medjugorje.

On one occasion Jesus spoke thus: "Father, Lord of heaven and earth, to you I offer praise; for what you have hidden from the learned and the clever you have revealed to the merest children. Father, it is true. You have graciously willed it so." [Matt. 11:25-26]

2

The Never-Ending Process

"I want to call you to start living a new life as of today. Dear children, I want you to comprehend that God has chosen each one of you, in order to use you in a great plan for the salvation of mankind. You are not able to comprehend how great your role is in God's design. Therefore, dear children, pray so that in prayer you may be able to comprehend what is God's plan through you. I am with you in order that you may be able to bring it about in all its fullness."—January 25, 1987

The message above given by the Blessed Virgin Mary at Medjugorje, focuses on the true meaning of conversion: each one of us is to play a definite and significant role in the plan of salvation for mankind as designed by God. That role is to be carried out each day of our lives.

To me conversion is absolute surrender—choosing God's will over one's own—trusting and obeying Him implicitly—cheerfully serving Him in whatever capacity He gives us. . . The process begins to unfold within each of us. And it never ends.

Many times it requires extraordinary spiritual and physical effort to carry the crosses given on the road to conversion; many times we are asked to also carry the crosses of our brothers and sisters. The guidelines are found in the Gospel messages of Matthew, Mark, Luke and John—in the living words of Jesus.

This is the essence of the thousands of messages given by Our Lady during the past ten years at this small mountain village: we are to *live* in ongoing spiritual conversion by learning to truly pray with the heart; to willingly fast at least once a week as a gift of self-denial and love for God; and, to practice penance by loving our neighbors in thought, word and deed.

Conversion means to change from one course of action to another. The course of action offered to us is prayer, fasting, and loving and caring for our neighbor. By these acts we live the messages daily from seemingly insignificant things to the major events in our lives.

I thought I *had* converted after receiving that beautiful personal call to devote my life to spreading the Medjugorje message. In the eight months between that moment and my personally going to the little village, I had learned to pray for more than just the automatic offering at mealtime or before sleep; I began to study early Church history; I learned more about apparitions; and, I began slowly trying to apply the steps she had so carefully laid out for us.

But on the first evening in Medjugorje, as I squeezed my way into a packed St James Church and immersed myself in the holiness and emotion of this miracle, I realized that my conversion had only been in its infancy. Being there, among several thousand who felt the same as I did, was the true, hands-on beginning.

And it was crystalized for me when this elderly woman from the village stood up and insisted that I take her seat on the crowded pew. Her weather-beaten, wrinkled face, streaked with tears of joy became for me a permanent sign of living conversion.

On that first pilgrimage I discovered that the entire village had been converted into a daily example of what God asks of us. Their quiet, secluded way of life had been changed forever, to serve as an example for the rest of the world. Their role, individually and collectively, was— and is—to serve the millions of pilgrims who come to Medjugorje. They have done so willingly. It is the same thing being asked of each of us.

In the years since receiving that message and attempting to say yes to God, I have also learned that there are indeed many crosses. Thousands of crosses. Crosses that I, and all who are touched by Medjugorje, are asked to share or pray for relief for the cross-bearer. The act of doing so is a very important part of conversion.

"Today I am calling you to decide if you wish to live the messages I am giving you. I wish you to be active in living and transmitting the messages."—June 5, 1986

Conversion affects each of us in a unique way. Recently I received this letter from a young woman named Mary Rose from New York:

Dear Mr. Weible,
First, let me tell you I am 24 years old, Catholic and have never really had the patience to sit down and read a book. I am more intrigued by activities such as participation in sports or games. However, I buried myself in your book and finished it in about a week.
When my sister Madeline showed me her copy of your book, I stared at the picture on the cover.

My eyes immediately filled up with tears, before I even read a word or knew anything about this great miracle that was happening. All I find myself talking about is Medjugorje, and the warm feeling I've had since learning about it.

I spoke in detail about Medjugorje with my boyfriend, Nick, who is Greek Orthodox. He couldn't wait to read your book. We have been going together for a year now and feel we will get married. However, our religion ideals were in conflict. A couple of weeks ago, I asked him when we get married what faith our children would be raised in. He was firm that our children were going to be Greek Orthodox and that would be final. I agreed to this with many reservations.

But my feelings later were growing stronger and stronger and I felt that God really didn't want that. He wanted me to confront him and stand my ground. I don't know if you know any Greeks but let me tell you, they are very stubborn. I really thought God was putting me through a great test to choose Him over Nick. I was torn inside for days.

Last night I finally confronted Nick and told him that I couldn't do it. I gave him many reasons why I think our children should be Catholic. The way our conversation started, it didn't sound like I was going to get what I wanted, but suddenly, Nick just totally changed his mind and said it was okay and that our kids could be baptized Catholic. I couldn't believe it! Usually when he makes up his mind, he will not budge.

I am certain that God is responsible for Nick's change of heart! I stood up for God, and He stood by me. What a feeling! Yesterday was Sunday and I went to Mass. In the Gospel (reading) it said to "say no when you mean no and yes, when you mean yes." I felt that it confirmed what I had to do. Maybe this is part of my conversion.

God bless you for what you are doing. I'm trying to help spread the message myself. By the way, I feel comfortable calling you "Wayne," because I feel I know you already.

Thank you for taking the time to read this.

Warmest regards,
Mary Rose

New York

Thinking about her letter, I prayed for the right words to say to her—as I do with each letter I feel requires an answer.

Dear Mary Rose,

Thank you for your letter and the testimony of your strong faith. You have indeed heard the call of Medjugorje, and I believe God gave you the strength to do what you had to do and remain true to your faith.

I also want you to know that when I first received that picture of Our Lady on the cover of my book, I, too, burst into tears. Something inside of me confirmed that it was a special mystical gift to us. That is why I felt that Our Lady asked me to use it on the cover of the book.

I will keep you in my prayers and ask that you do the same for me and my family. May Jesus and Mary always guide you and your future family in holiness.

In Christ,
Wayne

"Dear children, I have come to call the world to conversion

for the last time. Later, I will not appear any more on this earth."—May 2, 1982

Dear Mr. Weible,

During a recent trip to the United States, I attended Mass at Our Lady of Solitude, in Palm Springs. Attending simply out of duty, and being in a rather confused state of mind regarding my faith, I was surprised at my positive reaction to the story of Fatima, which was related by the priest during the homily. On my return to Canada, I started looking for books on Fatima. During the search your book was also recommended.

Being a relatively recent convert to Catholicism, I have always balked at the thought of confession, penance, the rosary and the devotion to Our Lady. These are, of course, among the key elements of the faith! Having read your book and the books on Fatima, I feel so drawn towards Our Blessed Lady, that my objections to these things have been effortlessly dismissed.

I cannot remember a time when I have felt so spiritually charged, and although I cannot confess to having heard voices, I do feel compelled to spread the message of Medjugorje. The problem is that given the ups and downs that have been characteristic of my faith life to date, I'm scared that this "high" might only be temporary. For this reason I'm scared to go public until I'm satisfied that this is indeed a permanent change.

However, there is a difference this time. My newly found devotion for our Blessed Lady has given me a clear focus that I have never had before. I believe that Her tears of grief will always compel me to fight my complacency.

Yours truly,

Sam

British Columbia, Canada

Dear Sam,

Thank you for your beautiful letter. It is difficult to admit even to oneself that we might backslide in our faith.

Sam, please understand that even though the miraculous events of Fatima and Medjugorje seem to have drawn you into a new surge of strength in your faith, it was you who opened your heart to receive it. Without your exercising the gift of free will, it would not have happened.

I assure you that the same gift will aid you in maintaining it so that you can "go public" and let others know by the way you live and by your witness, what God can do in our lives when we let Him.

And of course, your love of Mary will always sustain you. Pray the rosary and continue to search and you will stay on the right path.

May Jesus and Mary always guide you and your family.

In Christ,

Wayne

"Hurry to be converted. Do not wait for the great sign. For the unbelievers, it will be too late to be converted. For you who have the faith, this time constitutes a great opportunity for you to be converted, and to deepen your faith."—April 4, 1983

A school teacher from New Hampshire wrote the following letter. Normally I will not quote entire letters in this book, as many are quite long. But Shirley's was typical of so many, and so encouraging on the path of conversion, that it is included here almost in its entirety:

Dear Wayne,

For the past few months I have been moved again and again to write to you and tell you what has happened in my life since first becoming aware of the events of Medjugorje. Your writings have been instrumental in keeping alive the desire to know the messages and to apply them to my life.

I first read of Medjugorje three years ago in an article that appeared in Reader's Digest. I was having breakfast alone and was browsing through an old magazine when I saw the article. As I read it, I "felt" an urgent message inside me to go to my room. I think this may have been similar to what you experienced.

I went to my room and as I entered I felt that I was in the presence of someone or something, though I could see no one. I was flooded with a sense of awe. I felt as though grace was being poured over me. I was humbled and filled with the desire to know God in a more meaningful way. From that point on, I began to search for information about Medjugorje and the apparitions.

I read several books as the months passed. I found your newspaper articles in the back of our church one day and devoured the contents. I was particularly impressed because you were a Protestant and Medjugorje had made a profound impact on your life. I believed absolutely that what I was reading was truth, and yearned to make the trip to Medjugorje, though I knew this to be an impossibility because of my financial circumstances as a single parent.

My ongoing curiosity led me to hear speakers who had made the trip and one in particular who told me to "Ask the Mother of God, and it will happen." I did ask the Mother of God many times but did not foresee that it would ever happen.

Last April (1989), I went on a trip to Columbia, Maryland, to visit a friend. We toured Washington D. C. during the four days I was there and on the last day we made a visit to the Cathedral of the Immaculate Conception. I was deeply moved by the experience. We visited the gift shop and I sensed that there was something in this shop I should get. I chuckled to myself and said a quick prayer for guidance (I was getting used to following these urges!).

When I turned the corner, there was a display of your book, and I knew what I was supposed to buy. When I got outside of the shop I showed it to my friend who was not familiar with the story and I began to tell her about it. I was not far into the story when she stopped me by saying that she thought she had heard something about it and had a video tape at home that one of her friends had sent her. She had not seen the whole thing and asked if I might like to see it.

The tape made a deep impression on me. I realized that I was caught up in Medjugorje, and it was speaking to my heart. I shared my feelings with my friend and we shared beliefs with one another.

I left the next morning to return to New Hampshire. Midway through my journey a woman sat down beside me. She pulled out a Walkman and put on headphones. We sat there side by side, me with your book and she with her tape.

About half an hour later, she took off her headphones and turned to me and said, "Have you ever been to Medjugorje?" I told her that I had never been but wanted very much to go. She then told me about a friend of hers who had gone and whose life had changed by the experience. She said she envied her friend who was a Catholic, and that Medjugorje probably wouldn't do anything for her because she was a Protestant.

It was a wonderful opportunity for me to show her your book and the fact that you were not Catholic and yet the events had made a profound change in your life. I shared some of the messages with her and told her that they were for all of humanity.

At the end of August, I received a gift that was beyond my wildest dreams: a trip to Medjugorje with all expenses paid!

The trip is scheduled for December 28 through January 3, the only possible time I could go because I am a school teacher. I know this trip will be part of the incredible experiences that have happened over these months. I know I am being called there. I do not know why, but I am not questioning it. I feel I am being asked to step out in faith and do whatever it is that needs to be done.

I know that it is important for me to write this and send it to you; that somehow you are a part of it, too. Thank you for listening to me.

Sincerely,
Shirley

New Hampshire

"Dear children, I beseech you, surrender to the Lord your entire past, all the evil that has accumulated in your hearts.—February 25, 1987

Everyone needs God, but perhaps no group is more needy than those who are behind bars. In the several prison visits in my travels, I experienced, through the stories and sharing with the prisoners, that it is one of the hardest roads of conversion. They learn the harsh reality of not living God's love; they become cross-bearers after having created crosses for others. And, for those who admit their errors, ask forgiveness and seek a better way, they become some of the most fervent followers after discovering God's love.

Hello Wayne,

[This is] from all the guys in our Queen of Peace Prison Rosary Group. Your visit here at Southern State Prison was an answer to our group's prayer.

Many of our group members have been released back onto the streets, and I personally feel are armed not with guns, knives or dirty needles, but with true hope in Our Lady's messages and a purpose in life to carry them to others. Three guys out of the last seven released have written me back and keep me posted of their progress out there, and are working, attending different AA and or NA groups, as well as praying the rosary. Many of us have been witnesses to the power of prayer.

Now for my request: please keep me and our rosary group in your prayers to Our Lady, and please send me volume five of "Poem of the Man-God" for our group. You are in our prayers and in my heart. Thank you for sharing and caring.

Your brother in Christ,

Jim

Southern State Prison, N.J.

"Today I am calling you to holiness. Without holiness you cannot live. Therefore, with love overcome every sin, and with love overcome all the difficulties which are coming to you. Dear Children, I beseech you to live love within yourselves."—July 10, 1986

Last summer, I heard from a housewife named Stella, in North Carolina. As with the school-teacher Shirley, it is a long letter, but again most of it is included, because of the encouragement it offers:

Dear Wayne,

In my twenties, I met my future husband. We were engaged at 6:30 A.M. mass at the grotto of Our Lady of Lourdes at the Shrine of the Immaculate Conception in Washington, D.C. At the time we were very close to God. Afterwards, our relationship with God and our marriage deteriorated, though we spent 20 years trying to make it work. I had considered divorce, then resigned myself to having a life for myself while still married. Toward the end I had little faith.

On May 3, 1985, my husband had a massive life-threatening brain hemorrhage, the type that one rarely survives. That night as he lay in intensive care, I held his hand and talked to him most of the night. I told him how much I loved him. Despite everything, we always loved each other. Some of our happiest times were when I came to visit him (in the hospital during recovery).

My husband walked out of that hospital. The physical therapy continued at home. Despite all that had happened, our three children, then ages 18, 16, and 12, were wonderful to him. We treated him normally and we took him out with us even though he had these handicaps.

What I had never expected, and what had been my husband's greatest fear all his life was that he would become crazy. He did. His behavior was affected and he began to abuse the children. He convinced his doctor and others that we were abusing him. Fortunately, the person investigating realized that he was the abuser.

Our children really suffered from this. The night I had to take our middle one to the emergency room, I decided to file for divorce. Five days later, I did. We left the Midwest and came to North Carolina. I was now free to live the (sinful) life that appeared to be so much fun, and I did.

In 1988, I read about a trip to Fatima. I immediately signed up to fulfill a childhood dream of going there. Thereafter, I had second thoughts but decided I needed the vacation. At Kennedy Airport while at Mass, I was wondering what I was doing there with all those good Christian people. I felt out of place.

After we arrived our group went to the chapel located where Mary had appeared. I did not want

to go, but did since I had come so far. There, I
had a very emotional experience. I felt the
overwhelming presence of Mary.

I began to feel again, and with it suffered tremendous, unbearable pain. I went to prayer
groups and that helped some. After months of living in hell, and looking for some relief from all
this, I finally returned to some of my old ways (of
sin). I was still very unhappy.

It took me two years to have the courage to go
to Medjugorje (after hearing about it). I
subconsciously expected a lot. It took us two days
to get there and we missed our European flight.
So, we were only there for three days. It was not a
good trip. There were too many distractions. I felt
the main interest of the Yugoslavs was American
money. (But,) I was ready to stay when it was time
to return home!

I heard about the Medjugorje Conference in
New Orleans in December of 1990, and I wanted
to go, but not really—too many obstacles. All of
the impossible obstacles disappeared and two of
us drove 13 hours. I felt Mary wanted me to go
there, but I sure did not know why. I was
exhausted before I left.

It was the most fantastic experience of my life!
During the Eucharist, I raised my hands as the
priest does, and felt a pulsating in the middle of
my palms. I heard my heart say that yes, I would
surrender my life to Christ, and live the message.
I felt a burning sensation in my left eye. I have
had lots of eye problems in the last year, and I
finally feel at peace. I know now I substituted the
world's desires for God.

This was not an emotional experience that will

be short- lived. I have had a change of heart. All I
want to do is go out and spread the message.

Sincerely,

Stella

North Carolina

*"I have come to tell the world that God is Truth; He exists.
True happiness and the fullness of life are in Him. I have come
here as Queen of Peace to tell the world that peace is necessary
for the salvation of the world. In God, one finds true joy from
which peace is derived."—June 16, 1983*

I looked at the flight attendant on our Pan Am flight
home from Medjugorje in early spring of '91, and
immediately thought, "This lady could use a good dose
of Medjugorje."

She didn't appear to be too happy and in fact, struck
me exteriorly as hard and very much of the world. I thought
to myself, how she would change if only she knew about
Medjugorje, and some of the wonderful things that have
happened to people who have been there. Almost as if
reading my thoughts, she suddenly approached our seats.

Smiling, she asked if there was anything we needed
and casually asked where we had been. It was more than
just polite conversation or fulfillment of duty; she was
sincere and had a warm smile. I had the uneasy realization
that I had judged her strictly by appearance, in relation
to my own conversion—a classic example of spiritual
arrogance!

When she heard that we were returning from a week
in Medjugorje, and before we could explain any more,
she exclaimed in great excitement, "Oh, I've been there!

I believe in it strongly and talk about it with other people all the time!"

Suddenly, she looked at me and said, "My gosh, you're Wayne Weible! And this must be your family!"

I had a sick feeling in the pit of my stomach for having judged this woman without knowing anything about her. In no time we were involved in an animated conversation that would continue off and on throughout the eight-hour flight. In fact, her entire break times were spent in a squatting position in the cramped aisle of the airplane, talking to my wife Terri about how it had affected her life. She had had her share of crosses, but had gained the peace and strength to overcome them by learning the ways of conversion to God.

Sometimes, those of us who feel that we have reached some advanced level of conversion tend to become spiritually proud and a bit aloof. We sadly judge and then condemn those who "are of the world," forgetting that we were once there—and but for the grace of God would be there still. We suddenly become experts in the field of spirituality and see ourselves as capable and correct interpreters of Scripture. We feel "sorry" for those who cannot share that feeling. And from this, we judge; we do not practice mercy.

When we realize what we have done, it should be a strong indication to us that conversion is a never-ending process.

He summoned the crowd with his disciples and said to them: "If a man wishes to come after me, he must deny his very self, take up his cross, and follow in my steps. Whoever would preserve his life will lose it, but whoever loses his life for my sake and the gospel's will preserve it. What profit does a man show who gains the whole world and destroys himself in the process?" [Mark 8:34-36]

3

"With prayer you can stop wars..."

"Today, I invite you in a special way to pray for peace. Dear children, without peace, you cannot experience the birth of the Child Jesus neither today nor in your daily lives. Therefore, pray to the Lord of Peace that He may protect you with His mantle; and that He may help you to comprehend the greatness and the importance of peace in your hearts. In this way, you shall be able to spread peace from your hearts throughout the whole world.

I am with you and I intercede for you before God. Pray, because Satan wants to destroy my plan of peace. Be reconciled with one another, and by means of your lives work that peace may reign in the whole earth."—December, 1990.

One of the greatest examples of the miraculous power of prayer—especially for peace—was given to us during the recent Persian Gulf War. How is it possible to assemble a huge allied army of more than half a million men and women, undertake a furious-paced air offensive, launch an expected bloody ground campaign—and come away decisively victorious with less than 250 mortal casualties?

Granted, even one loss of life is too much, for war is the total absence of God's love, and the dark presence of Satan's hatred for mankind. Yet, such variance in numbers leaves us with a modern-day example of how God's armies of the Old Testament not only survived but won just battles against great odds. They won because they went to their knees as a nation devoted to Him and prayed.

From the early months of confrontation in late 1990, until the quick end of the ground campaign, people all over the world were on their knees fervently and tirelessly praying for world peace. They prayed long and often. And God listened.

People have asked me, what about the Iraqis—doesn't God love them, too? Of course He does! But they chose to follow an evil leader. And they could not be allowed to simply take another country because they wanted it. Where would the conquest end?

Saddam Hussein was appealed to, pleaded with, prayed for. I personally know dozens of people who were actually praying for his conversion—including myself. But he was totally committed to an evil course. And God does not force any man to do His will, even when that man is a leader who by his actions is condemning followers to the loss of thousands of lives.

The Blessed Virgin Mary at Medjugorje asked us in a pleading way to pray for world peace. In a unique message on January 25, 1991, she indicated how directly heaven is involved in world affairs by saying, *"Today, like never before, I invite you to prayer. Your prayer should be a prayer for peace. Satan is strong and wishes not only to destroy human life but also nature and the planet on which you live. . ."*

What followed shortly thereafter was total confirmation of this urgent message. In the following 40 days, there was the ultimate build-up of forces in preparation for a predicted high-casualty land battle; the largest oil spill in history was deliberately released into the Persian Gulf in a horrendous act of ecological terrorism; and putrid black smoke created by nearly 600 oil wells maliciously set on fire engulfed the entire region.

Do we even now in its aftermath, grasp the intense seriousness of her asking us to pray "as never before"? It calls to mind part of an earlier message in which she said, *"With prayer, you can stop wars. . . and change the course of nature."*

As always, Mary was right: the war came to an abrupt and miraculous end.

But it needed people to believe her, when she said that prayer could stop wars. Enough believed, and enough prayed from the heart, and a miracle happened.

Another miracle, even bigger, happened in Eastern Europe. Seventy years of Communism—of godless rule—collapsed in a matter of weeks. How did this happen? Some might say it was Gorbachev's glasnost or perestroika. Others might credit President Reagan's toughness or diplomatic initiative. But there have been Summit meetings and Salt talks for years, and nothing ever came of them. There is another answer: prayer.

Is it coincidence that the Blessed Mother in her messages at Medjugorje continually calls us to pray for world peace? Is it also coincidence that for nine years people from the Eastern European countries have trekked to Medjugorje by bus, by train, by car—and many on foot—and returned to their countries with new hope for freedom and peace? Is it coincidence that the revolutions which brought down Communism in Poland, in Hungary, in Czechoslovakia, in Romania—in Yugoslavia — began in the churches, with people on their knees?

No. The visionaries have reported that the Blessed Virgin Mary has stated in her messages that the prayer, fasting, and penance of those who have come to Medjugorje have had a profound effect on the recent changes in Eastern Europe.

Once again, in this time of continuing world crisis, Mary is calling on us to employ the greatest of all spiritual tools, prayer. And it is to be applied to the other "wars" — those that rage within families and between individuals and within ourselves. It is to be applied to the wars that continue against the evil of abortion, drugs and family abuse.

She says we are to pray for peace—not only peace in the world, but peace within ourselves. There should also be prayers for world leaders, for protection against natural disasters and for protection of nature and the planet on which we live. Oil spills, smoke-filled skies and devastated land that will be scorched for years is the inheritance of the non- love of God. That is the condition that creates wars of all kinds.

Mary asks us to "grasp the rosary." She reminds us over and over at Medjugorje that this beautiful prayer will allow us to relive Jesus' life and to pattern our lives after His through its constant lesson.

After all, that is the reason she has come to us at Medjugorje: that we might learn the ways of holiness.

As the beautiful mother of Jesus tells us over and again, we must pray, pray, pray!

"Dear children, pray as much as you can, pray how you can, pray more and more. When I tell you to pray, pray, pray, you must understand it is not just an increase in the numbers of prayers. I want to bring you to a deep desire for God, that you may always desire God." —to the young people in Jelena's prayer group, February, 1984.

Dear Wayne,
    Before I go any further, forgive me for taking up so much of your time on reading this letter. I

do know how busy a person your are but could you please bear with me?

I was given this newspaper, "Miracles at Medjugorje" by a friend. After reading it, I said that I had to write to you and tell you about Ryan, my grandson.

Ryan is autistic. He can't talk, is not toilet-trained, can't remember when taught. He screams, never sits down, and he walks for miles. He goes to an autistic school. This school has government cutbacks so this one-to-one contact for these kids is taken away. He was showing such improvement, but now this year he is not showing any improvement.

Wayne, what's happening to my family? I could not be loved by Jesus, Mary and Joseph. Let me put you in the picture: 1) Wendy, (that's Ryan's mother) has had boils for the past 17 years and has not found a cure; 2) Marc, Ryan's oldest brother is a chronic asthmatic, he can't leave home after 6 PM as he gets a bad attack of asthma; 3) Ryan is also asthmatic; 4) my second daughter's husband, Brian, has had a kidney transplant and now after three years (the kidney) is being rejected.

What do we do with a situation like this? We are being crushed to the ground! It's hard work for Wendy and Rick. Ryan wrecks the house and his room.

Now, this is where you come in. Could you please ask any of these children that Our Lady appeared to, to request them to pray to Our Lady for Ryan, for his brain to start to work as a normal brain, to talk, to calm down and to toilet-train?

There is no future for Ryan. When he is 15 years old, he will be put away. O my God, how could we do this? Our Lady would have to plead to Jesus for a Miracle. Wayne, do something for Ryan. Put this letter at Our Lady's feet. Think of Ryan as your son. Something has got to happen for him.

Wayne, do you know Sister Briege McKenna? She has a personal gift (of healing) from God. Could you ask her to pray for Ryan? Thank you, Wayne, for your precious time.

God love you always,
Doris

Western Australia

Dear Doris,

I want you to know that I have been praying for Ryan and for his entire family.

Doris, it is difficult to understand at times, but Ryan is a gift to your family. With Ryan's disability your family must work closer together to take care of his needs and that alone gives you the courage to go on. Prayer—and strong belief in what prayer can achieve—is the daily medicine needed for Ryan and for each member of the family.

I will pray for peace to fill the hearts of each of you; I will pray especially for a healing for Ryan, but most especially for Ryan's family to stand together and accept Ryan as he is. In other words, for submission to what God wants in his life and out of his life.

May Jesus and Mary give you strength to accept what is given in life.

In Christ,
Wayne

Dear Wayne,

Thank you for your letter. You have given me something to look forward to. Wayne, my grandson is showing some improvement!

In his December report (from his special school), the remarks were so lovely. His teacher writes out the children's name and makes them pick out their name. Ryan now picks up his name and gives it to his teacher. He also swims (self-taught) and goes under the water.

Now there is some trouble in the camp (school) and the government says it may have to close it and there will be no place like this for autistic children. Please continue to pray for Ryan and the other children.

Yours sincerely,
Doris

Western Australia

"Dear Children: Today, I want to call you to pray, pray, pray! In prayer you will come to know the greatest joy and the way out of every situation. Thank you for moving ahead in prayer."—March 29, 1985

Perhaps the most moving letters I receive—and the most humbling—are those which give an indication of how God is using the talks to His glory. His, not mine—if I ever thought I had anything personally to do with it, I would quit and go home. All I do is go where He sends me, say what He asks me to say, and write what He asks me to write. Whatever else happens is up to Him. But occasionally as an encouragement (I need them, as everyone does), I receive letters like this one:

Dear Wayne,

Prior to your speech date at St Raphael's, I battled with a recurring corneal abrasion/erosion, which was in a vulnerable state due to the extensive scar tissue of the cornea. I am a nurse, and therefore was aware of possible surgery. I am also very close to Our Lady; therefore, I asked for one request "to hear and feel Medjugorje."

The morning of your talk I (was able to do this, which normally would not have been possible) removed the eye patch for two hours, then again at 6 PM (that evening).

I was moved at St Raphael's, not especially by Wayne Weible, but more importantly, through Mary's love. I nearly fainted when your voice echoed in my ear, "I'm glad you're here." That was Mary's love.

Just prior to your talk, a strong inner voice urged me to pray the fifth Glorious Mystery, which is the fruit—trust in Mary's intercession. I finished the decade as the applause silenced.

This past weekend, I was walking in the Blue Ridge Mountains, listening to a tape of your talk (given at St James Church in Medjugorje), when again Mary prompted me to write you this note; my inner spirit (or Mary) wants me to keep you in my prayers to strengthen you against adversities. I really don't understand but this does happen frequently; therefore, I follow this loving ministry without question.

I am a regular person like you. My children are young and my husband is in school. But, we are alike in our love and close relationship with

Mother Mary. Take good care of yourself and
Terri, (and) don't forget to savor your family's love.

Love,

Judy

North Carolina

Another time, I was in a little town outside of Pittsburgh,
and I had just completed a talk on the beautiful apparitions
of Medjugorje to an overflow crowd jammed into a
magnificent old church. Prayer and its powerful effects on
restoring families had been the center of this particular talk.

As I came off the altar I was greeted by a woman visibly
distressed. She grabbed my arm and pulled me aside before
others in the crowd could say anything. "Please, Wayne,
please," she cried, "You've got to help me. My son is on
drugs and is always into some kind of trouble. He doesn't
attend church anymore or spend much time with his
family—please pray for him; ask the Blessed Mother to
ask Jesus to heal him."

Before I could answer, a young man grabbed the woman
by the arm and said, "Listen, lady, don't stop praying for
him yourself! My mom prayed for me for *ten years*, because
I was addicted to all kinds of drugs and in and out of
jail. Now I'm here in church! I love Jesus! He healed
me! And it's because my mom never gave up on me!"

Stunned by this outburst, the woman thanked the young
man and walked away. I did not need to say a thing.

*Dear children, today, I am calling you to prayer. Without prayer
you cannot feel me, nor God, nor the graces I am giving you.
Therefore, I call you always to begin and end each day with
prayer. Dear children, I wish to lead you evermore in prayer,
but you cannot grow because you don't want it. I invite you
to let prayer have the first place. — July 3, 1986*

Dear Mr. Weible,

Our Lady has blessed and touched your life completely and she has also touched mine. I was in Medjugorje in April of this year (1990) and my life has not been the same since.

I know how you feel when you said on your tape you did not want to leave Medjugorje. I pray someday I can go back again but now I am trying to spread the message. I am a Catholic and I love Our Lady and Jesus with all my heart. My husband and I have been married for 30 years and have five beautiful children.

Wayne, please remember my son in your prayers. He is married and 23 years old. He has Jesus in his heart but does not believe in Mary. You see, he does not go to a Catholic church anymore, and where he goes, they don't believe in Mary or the saints. I have told him about Medjugorje but he still does not believe. I pray the rosary all the time and all I ask him is to open his eyes and heart to our mother, Mary. I am not asking him to come back to our faith—only to open his heart to Mary. Please pray for him.

Thank you,
Betty

Ohio

"You wonder why all these prayers? Look around you, dear children, and you will see how greatly sin has dominated this earth. Pray, therefore, that Jesus conquers."—September 13, 1984

Dear Wayne,

I have always been interested in the phenomenon of Medjugorje. Even though I have never been there I do believe.

I just have one request. My wanting a miracle of my husband's disease (chronic polyneuropathy, Multiple Sclerosis) has gotten me quite upset, frustrated and angry with the doctors who are allegedly taking care of him. See, he has been paralyzed (limbs) off and on for two years with no real diagnosis.

I have also, along with Gregg, my husband, and his parents, been praying for a healing of whatever he has. I have now come to the conclusion that if we just find out what he has, we can go from there.

Would you please just pray for Gregg, for a healing of whatever he has? I know you are busy so I want to thank you very, very much, for God is truly with you.

God's love,
Dianne

Indiana

"Today I invite you all so that your prayer be a prayer with the heart. Let each of you find time for prayer so that in your prayer you discover God. I do not desire you to talk about prayer, but to pray. Let your every day be filled with prayers of gratitude to God for life and for all that you have. I do not desire your life to pass by in words but that you glorify God with deeds. I am with you and I am grateful to God for every moment spent with you."—April 25, 1991

Dear Wayne,

Your book has renewed a very strong faith in my heart and soul, that somewhere along the line seemed to weaken.

Many years ago I asked if there was really a God, or if Jesus was really there. In a prayer, of which I'm not too good at, I asked Him to please help me. I was alone, but what I saw and felt on that day seventeen years ago, no one could take from me.

I have no religion, but I read the Bible and go to church when I can. I believe that with our Lord, all things are possible because He has helped me out more times than I deserve.

God bless you and your family and keep you safe and healthy to continue God's blessed works.

Thank you, again
Sharon

Idaho

Visionary Ivan Dragicevic undertook his first speaking tour in the United States in late 1990. He spent many wonderful days in high schools and evenings in churches, discussing the events of Medjugorje. I am struck by the maturity which has come to this young man, even in the few short years I have known him. The boy who had run away the first day that Our Lady appeared on the side of the hill, runs no more.

Ivan speaks boldly and wisely now. He speaks mostly to youth groups, and during his tour, the power of prayer was usually the main subject of his messages. Here are a few excerpts:

"In the first year of the apparitions we prayed as the Mother of God taught us. But compared with today, it was then still on a low level. We tried to translate into life all that Our Lady told us. The Mother of God leads us into a prayer so deep that this prayer penetrates all the pores of our lives. It forms us into people of strong character. She has thanked us often for our help. This, for me, is something so great that I cannot grasp it, that we sinners can help Her through our prayers. . ."

"We pray with our hearts. That is true prayer. If we pray with our heart we experience every word that we utter. We ponder the words and each one penetrates our soul and forms us spiritually. During one encounter [apparition] the Mother of God gave me the following message: *'One Our Father prayer should take three minutes in order to be prayed as it should be.'* It was then that I started to pray with my heart. I had prayed before, but not as deeply."

At one high school, Ivan even had an apparition in front of the more than 1,200 students. And that evening, as is so often the case, the message for the youth was to pray. At another school in Pennsylvania, more than 1,500 students remained after Ivan's talk to voluntarily pray the full fifteen decades of the rosary.

In almost every message the Blessed Virgin has given at Medjugorje, She asks for prayer. It is, without doubt, the most powerful spiritual weapon we have today.

At every opportunity pray in the Spirit, using prayers and petitions of every sort. Pray constantly and attentively for all in the holy company. [Eph. 6:18]

4

Fasting, a Gift to God

"I thank you for all your prayers. I thank you for all your sacrifices. I wish to tell you, dear children, to renew the messages I am giving you. Especially live the fasting, because with fasting you will give me joy for the fulfillment of all God's plan here in Medjugorje." — *September 26, 1985*

Of all the things Mary asks of us at Medjugorje, the request for fasting is probably the hardest to put into practice and carry out on a daily basis. For most of us, it is difficult to fully understand, let alone accept. Not by coincidence have I received fewer letters on fasting than on other subjects in this book. But while this may be one of the shortest chapters, it is also one of the most important.

Fasting is out of step with our times. We're too busy; it doesn't fit in with work schedules and activities. And there's too much abundance surrounding us, and the temptation is too great.

This is exactly why it is so essential to the successful implementation of the message of Medjugorje in daily living.

For many people their first experience with fasting was

when they went to Medjugorje. But, you might say, I didn't fast then.

You did, however, without being aware of it. You fasted from television. You fasted from the telephone and newspapers and magazines. And, you fasted from countless diversions and distractions of the modern world. While you were in Medjugorje, there was no "busyness," no idle chatter, no preoccupation with family or work.

The result was a new communion with God. You gave Him a gift: your undivided attention for a full week.

The entire purpose of fasting is to reinforce the spirit and put it in control of the flesh. It subdues the demand for instant gratification—whether it be food, pleasure, or sensuality. It steels us for what is to come in the purification of the world. It also allows us to give something back to God, a gift of our desire to live His way that can vary in value depending on our degree of commitment.

Some days it is a rich gift of strict bread and water— or just water; on other days, when it becomes a struggle due to the myriad of daily-life distractions, the gift of fasting may diminish in value—but not in effort.

There is so much to this gift that we can give to God! It isn't just about giving up rich foods for a day or two, or a week. We need to fast from the vast variety of conveniences offered to us through modern technology. And we need to fast from the flesh; that includes the sensual and the comfortable. The Blessed Virgin Mary confirms this in numerous messages from the early days of the apparitions right through the 1991 crisis of war in the Persian Gulf.

The first mention of fasting by the Virgin Mary came on the second day she appeared to the visionaries. Marija Pavlovic was making her way down the pathway towards the village after the initial apparition with the Madonna, having gone on ahead of the other five youngsters. It was a stifling hot late afternoon; two of the girls had become light-headed due to the excitement of the apparition and effects of the late-June heat. Suddenly, Our Lady appeared to Marija for the second time that afternoon, just ahead and to her left a few feet away. Standing there with a rainbow colored cross in her arms, she somberly implored Marija to pray in order to achieve individual peace: *"Peace, Peace, Peace! Be reconciled! Only peace. Make your peace with God and among yourselves. For that it is necessary to believe, to pray, to fast, and to go to confession."*

In the coming months the Lady from Heaven would emphasize continually the need to pray and fast, especially in times of great trial. She asked them to use fasting as a weapon against the power of evil, warning that Satan would try to impose his power on them: *"But you must remain strong and persevere in your faith. You have to pray and fast. I will always be close to you"* *(November, 1981);* it was also to be used for the sick and crippled: *"For the cure of the sick, it is important to say the following prayers: the Creed, and seven times each, The Lord's Prayer, the Hail Mary, and the Glory Be,—and to fast on bread and water."*— *July, 1982*

Some cannot fast on bread and water as requested by Mary. Those who are ill or perform heavy physical work— or those simply unable due to weakness of the spirit— have an option. Mary gave this message in December, 1981, after many villagers had slackened in their practice of fasting (as do many pilgrims after a few months of strong commitment): *"If you do not have the strength to fast on bread and water, you can give up a number of things. It would be a good thing to give up television, because after seeing some programs, you are distracted and unable to pray. You can give up alcohol, cigarettes and other pleasures. You yourselves know what you have to do."*

As stated earlier this very direct message confirms that fasting is more than taking one day a week and having only bread and water. It is a gift that incorporates full commitment only after a time of learning how and why to fast. Like any learning process, it takes patience, practice and perseverance.

The practice of "giving something" back to God is not new. The early members of the church fasted two days a week—Wednesdays and Fridays. The most zealous among them would also fast on Saturday, in preparation of Sunday services. By the third century the practice became more widespread and began to be kept for entire weeks. This then developed into the forty-day fasting period during Lent which is still practiced as a preparation for Easter. And of course the forty days represents the number of days Jesus fasted in the desert before His three-year public mission [Luke 4:1-4].

Bearing in mind these beautiful messages concerning fasting by Our Lady at Medjugorje, the next step is applying them. Like prayer, fasting is a powerful tool given its proper use. And when combined with prayer for a specific intention, it creates an atmosphere that can "stop wars and change the laws of nature."

"Dear children, today I call you to prepare your hearts for these days when the Lord particularly desires to purify you from all the sins of your past. You, dear children, are not able by yourselves, therefore, I am here to help you. You pray, dear children! Only that way shall you be able to recognize all the evil that is in you and surrender it to the Lord so the Lord may completely purify your hearts. Therefore, dear children, pray without ceasing and prepare your hearts in penance and fasting."—December 4, 1986

Dear Mr. Weible,

If I may, I have a question for you that I have never seen addressed in any Medjugorje publication. We first learned of Our Lady's messages (of fasting, etc.) in early 1983. It was said that She "asked us to fast on bread and water."

We later attended a Medjugorje conference and we left promising ourselves to follow the request for fasting. The following Friday, all seven of our family began the fast.

The children were in school so they were allowed a sandwich at lunch. Several years later, we began home schooling and bread all day (for all of us, including the children) was the norm.

In 1988, my husband and I went to Medjugorje, and while at Ivan's house to hear him speak with our group, he made the statement that children were not to fast. I could not understand how he could say that. We continued to fast once back home, even though my husband was in a deep depression.

This past year I've heard more about children not fasting, and to add to that, my children no longer want to fast. My question is this: would you please straighten me out on children fasting? (Mine are ages nine through 18). Also, should I tell them they no longer have to do it, or encourage them to continue?

It seems Satan is sitting on our shoulders lately. None of our kids seem to care about anything spiritual and I am beginning to wonder why I tried to impress on them (the need of) a spiritual life.

I know you hear this all the time, and I keep

thinking that somehow I am not seeing the help
Our Lady says she'll give us for the asking. Since
you are so blessed with doing so much for our
Heavenly Mother, I'm sure Satan is all over you.
I'm sorry to bother you with this question, but I
don't know who else to talk to about it.

God bless you and Mary keep you!

Sincerely,
Gerrianne

Missouri

Dear Gerrianne,

Please understand from the outset that those of us who
have committed our lives to the messages of Medjugorje,
will experience constant attack by the evil one. *His*
commitment is to destroy us individually and as families.
He does this best through our children.

Having heard Ivan speak on many occasions, I feel he
was referring to *small* children when he stated they should
not be included in a strict bread-and-water fast. The same
would apply to the elderly and sick. On the other hand,
young adults in their teens are fully capable of fasting
as well as comprehending its purpose.

It is, however, all too common for post-Medjugorje
pilgrims to come on too strong to family and friends,
especially in the beginning. And, the primary recipients
of this new-found spiritual zeal are usually spouses and/
or children. Too much, too soon can quickly turn them
off and push them in the opposite direction. And that
is when Satan is most able to subtly lead them into divisive
rebellion.

I would encourage you, therefore, to be the "gentle
mother," in imitation of Mary. By your own example lead
your children to God with love, tolerance, and patience.

Possibly it would be best to ask of them a fast on soup and sandwiches; that way it does not seem a punishment or task, but a way to give God a special gift. As they age and mature, the gift will improve voluntarily.

That is not to say you shouldn't point out the importance of spiritual conversion through fasting, as well as prayer. Also give examples from scripture readings how Jesus would fast and pray, especially in times of stress. Have open discussions with them as a family and find out the reasons they no longer wish to participate in weekly fasting, again, attempting to do so in a loving, understanding parental way.

At the same time, we must be reasonably firm as parents and enforce family rules as long as the children live in the same house. Too often parents are afraid of asserting their parental rights for fear of psychologically damaging their children. This mode of thinking comes to us over a period of years as a result of secular world intent on self-focus. The idea is to balance the two and come to a clear understanding as to why you ask them to fast.

Please know that I will keep you and your family in my prayers, praying especially that your entire family is able to persevere in following the Medjugorje messages of prayer and fasting.

In Christ,
Wayne

"The best fast is on bread and water. Through fasting and prayer, one can stop wars, one can suspend the laws of nature. Charity cannot replace fasting. Those who are not able to fast can sometimes replace it with prayer, charity and a confession; but everyone, except the sick, must fast." — July 21, 1982

We have already discussed how concentrated fasting and prayer can work wonders—as was seen in the Persian Gulf crisis. This was a crisis on the verge of becoming a world war. Millions of people of all faiths around the world were on their knees praying and studiously fasting for an end to the fighting and the establishment of real peace. It happened, and it happened quickly, with a miraculously low loss of life among Coalition Forces.

Another beautiful example of the powerful combination of prayer and fasting was related to me in 1989 by my sponsors in Singapore, Dr. Victor Wee, and his wife Vivienne. During a few quiet moments between engagements, we sat discussing how Medjugorje had affected us personally. It was then I learned of the beautiful story of how Victor's mother was converted.

Victor and Vivienne were already doing a great deal of what Our Lady is asking before ever making a pilgrimage to Medjugorje. They were involved in the marriage encounter program in their Catholic church, were devout in their faith, and had adopted a Downe's Syndrome child. All of this was, of course, additional to the full schedule of practicing medicine and assisting the poor in need of medical treatment.

"When we traveled to Medjugorje and heard the message, I knew immediately what I had to return home and do," Victor told me as we enjoyed a morning cup of coffee before setting out on a busy schedule of talks. "You see," he paused for a moment, "I have a mother who is in her eighties and whose health is very poor. At the time of our trip, she was also a professed atheist. The message and the mission for Vivienne and myself was clear to both of us: we had to fast and pray that my mother would find Jesus before her death."

I was surprised that one so deeply involved in living Jesus' Gospel message *before* going to Medjugorje, could have a mother who had no faith in God.

Victor proceeded with his story: "On the way home we determined to pray and fast with a definite purpose. Our immediate purpose was to do this for my mother. I knew she would not live much longer, and we wanted her to become a Christian and join the church before her death.

He smiled, and then said, "But when I told my mother that we intended to pray and fast for her so that she would know Jesus, she told us in no uncertain terms to mind our own business! If we wanted to chase such fairy tales, that was fine with her, but for us to leave her alone."

Of course we didn't. We did everything we could to love her and let her know how much we cared; with our fasts every Wednesday and Friday, we set as an intention her conversion to Jesus. Our kids joined us. With this kind of 'attack,' we knew it would work!"

Victor laughed, and squaring his chair around so that he was looking right at me, he added with that wonderful glow that comes from the eyes of those who have been touched by Medjugorje, "And do you know, within six months my mother joined the church!"

Ten months later, Victor's mother passed away, receiving the last rites of the Church and dying in the peace of Jesus.

"Observe the complete fasts, Wednesdays and Fridays. Pray at least an entire rosary: Joyous, Sorrowful and Glorious Mysteries."—August 14, 1985

One evening in Medjugorje, I was staying at the home of Marija, and we were sitting around the kitchen table, talking about fasting and how Americans in particular took it so seriously—and struggled to meet its demands.

"The thing is," I said to Kathleen, a young American who had been staying with Marija and assisting her with English-speaking pilgrims for the last two years, "Americans always try to do something like this from the very beginning as though they were perfectly able to do it without practice and past preparation."

"I know," she replied, "They try and fail, and then they quit living that part of the message."

I smiled as I recalled how my own wife Terri had come home from her first trip to Medjugorje, determined to fast strictly on bread and water. No butter for her; no jams or hot tea or coffee—strictly bread and water. It finally came to the point that the kids and I *begged* her not to fast. We couldn't take it! She was irritable and ill and it took her all of the next day to recover. Later, after much prayer and practice, she became the example for us to follow, routinely fasting on Wednesdays and Fridays.

"Yes, I know all too well what you're saying," I laughed thinking about Terri and many others who asked me about fasting during the speaking tours. "Many people admit they fast on bread and water all day, but the moment the clock strikes midnight, they make a mad dash for the refrigerator!"

Kathleen looked at me and burst out laughing so hard she could hardly speak, finally gasping, "Oh, Marija and I do that all the time!"

I've never forgotten that lesson. When I fast, I like to go through to breakfast. So that word, which literally means "breaking the fast of the night," twice a week means two nights and a day to me. Fasting is a personal gift. It is gift of varying value depending on the person and the preparation and the point of conversion. Whether it is plain bread and water, or one with a little jelly or peanut butter it is an effort to give back to God something of value.

It comes down to realizing once again that we can't give these gifts to God on our own; when we try to do it without His Grace, it usually fails. For it is grace that allows us to offer Him a gift and draw closer to His love. It becomes a lesson in humility; the humble heart of a child is able to offer a simple gift that is great in the eyes of God.

Thus, you might say that fasting is akin to mothers and dads receiving those beautiful crayon-colored scribblings of pictures from their little children. We're thrilled when our little ones give us such gifts of love. So is God when we give Him the gift of fasting.

"Dear children, pray for the gift of love, for the gift of faith, for the gift of prayer, for the gift of fasting!" — *April 17, 1986.*

When you fast, your are not to look glum as the hypocrites do. They change the appearance of their faces so that others may see they are fasting. I assure you, they are already repaid. When you fast, see to it that you groom your hair and wash your face. In that way no one can see you are fasting but your Father who is hidden; and your Father who sees what is hidden will repay you. [Matt. 6:16-18]

5

Penance, Responding to the gifts

"Dear children, today I invite you to give thanks to God for all the gifts you have discovered in the course of your life and even for the least gift you have received. I give thanks with you and want all of you to experience the joy of these gifts, and I want God to be everything for each one of you. And then, little children, you can grow continuously on the way of holiness.."—September 25, 1989

Our Lady constantly talks about the gifts God has given us—the gift of conversion, the gift of prayer, the gift of fasting, and of course the millions of little gifts of daily life that we take for granted.

We have spoken of fasting as a gift to God. Like this gift, penance is a difficult concept to assimilate. Stated briefly, we might describe penance as our free will response in gratitude for the spiritual gifts God gives us. Often it is given in atonement for past sins, or in thanksgiving for discovering true peace. For those newly baptized in the unique spirituality of Medjugorje, it is frequently described as that "inner urge" which compels us to want to do something in return.

Unceasing prayer from the heart, coupled with once

or twice-a-week fasting with a definite intent sets the tone of the daily penance asked of us by the Blessed Virgin. It is the same commitment Jesus asks of each of us in His Gospel, and it is what our churches ask of us: to voluntarily give our love by word, thought and deed, and to desire the same in return.

The word penance usually is thought to be something hard to do, something negative. Yet when viewed as acts of love in response to love, it is wonderfully positive. It is the practice of virtue and mercy as described in Colossians 3:12-14—*Because you are God's chosen ones, holy and beloved, clothe yourselves with heartfelt mercy, with kindness, humility, meekness, and patience. Bear with one another; forgive whatever grievances you have against one another. Forgive as the Lord has forgiven you. Over all these virtues put on love which binds the rest together and makes them perfect.*

This penance—this *love in action*—feeds our spirituality. It brings with it an energy that enables families to bond together in times of crisis, to assist loved ones suffering with disabilities and terminal diseases. How often have we read of parents losing a child to drugs or some unknown disease, and then turning their efforts to a life-time working commitment, to prevent others from making the same mistakes? A terrible, single tragedy blossoms into a multitude of ongoing acts of charity. This penance is not a negative; it is a positive act of mercy and love.

For Medjugorje converts, responding to the message with acts of love should begin in the family—and there is not one family I know of that does not have one or more members suffering. Some suffer from the ravages of disease, disability and/or social addictions; others from broken relationships or abusive situations. This is where Mary Virgin calls us to begin our action of love. It is here where prayer from the heart, combined with fasting, must begin—for that family member who is in pain.

It is not always comfortable or easy; but if we are ever to obtain true peace and happiness, it must be done. Then, from responding to the cries of need from mother, father, brother, sister, we learn to do the same for our neighbor.

"Dear children, you cannot imagine what is going to happen nor what the Eternal Father will send to earth. That is why you must be converted! Renounce everything. Do penance. Express my thanks to all my children who have prayed and fasted. I carry all this to my Divine Son in order to obtain an alleviation of His justice against the sins of mankind."—June 24, 1983

Dear Wayne,

Just a short note to thank you. I was the man who sat next to you in the front row when you came to speak to us at our prison.

I am in here for "death by auto." This is my first time in jail and the last. I choose not to drink anymore. I belong to AA now.

This has given me a lot of time to take my inventory and do something about it. I enjoy prayer, and I pray a whole lot more sincere than ever before. I do not pray for anymore bargains with God or Mary. I pray for my guidance and all others.

This is like doing the sorrowful mysteries in here. Please pray for me.

Thank you and God bless,
John, from prison

St James wrote one letter to the early Church. In it he said that a double-minded man is unstable in all his ways

[1:8]. Penance is a wonderful means of closing a divided heart. When we are doing for others, it takes our minds off our own problems and inner conflicts.

In Medjugorje, Jelena, who receives inner-locutions, was shown a special vision—the tragedy of a divided heart.

"Jelena, man's heart is like this splendid pearl. When he belongs completely to the Lord, he shines even in the darkness. But when he is divided, a little to Satan, a little to sin, a little to everything, he fades and is no longer worth anything."—June, 1985

With this message, the Blessed Mother had shown Jelena an inner vision of a beautiful pearl which then divided into many pieces. Each section glittered for a few moments and then faded.

When our lives are divided into many pieces, and we desire to possess all that we can in the world, we fall into darkness. Prison is total darkness and involuntary penance. It is negative penance. Yet, as Our Lady points out in this unique message and example, when we repent and give ourselves entirely to God, He shines even in the darkness of a prison cell.

Dear Wayne,

Thank you for your efforts in spreading the messages of Medjugorje and in helping others to do so. What you are doing has meant a great deal to me and many others here in Sweden.

I am a career American diplomat with over 20 years service in Asia, Africa, and now Scandinavia. I first went to Medjugorje on my way to my present assignment at the American Embassy in Stockholm. After my 12 days in Medjugorje and the deep changes it brought me, I wondered what I was doing going to Sweden, where I had heard belief was minimal and anti-

Catholicism was still rampant.

I am so grateful to have discovered after a year and a half here that through Mary's grace and the power of her messages I have found more fulfillment than I had ever known, introducing people in Sweden to Medjugorje.

The receptivity here on the part of the Catholic minority, Lutherans and other Protestants, as well as non-believers, continues to surprise me. It seems further evidence that this is indeed a time of special grace. Although on a much smaller scale than what you are doing, this mission has become for me the most important aspect of my life right now. I am grateful for whatever opportunities are intrusted to me and I am ready to do whatever our Blessed Mother asks.

In the meantime, I find that inviting people to see your video and others is the most loving thing I can do for others. After a typical evening of sharing videos and my own experience, people who could not have conceived of apparitions by the Mother of God come away so grateful to have learned of Medjugorje. Nothing gives me greater pleasure than this.

I also tell them of the many beautiful signs that God has allowed Mary to give, especially what happened to me on the first of my four pilgrimages. Just before I left Medjugorje, I bought the first crucifix I had owned since my youth. Coming down from the Hill of Apparitions where I had brought it for Mary's blessing, I slipped on the muddy path and falling backward, struck the crucifix hard against a rock. Back in my room, I discovered that the crucifix was broken; a piece of wood had broken off the cross.

In Copenhagen, my rest stop on the way to
Stockholm, I thought about saying a rosary before
going out to eat. Although it was the hour that we
pray the rosary in Medjugorje, I felt like putting it
off until later. Concerned that I was already feeling lazy so soon after Medjugorje, I said a prayer
to Mary that she strengthen me in my commitment to pray. Then I took the broken crucifix out
of my suitcase—and saw that the missing piece of
wood had been restored and the cross was perfect
again! That was the happiest moment of my life
and I can never be grateful enough.

During the second international youth prayer
festival in August, 1990, at Medjugorje, Father
Tomislav said that those of us who want to give
ourselves completely to Jesus will have their
hearts filled with such love that we will be able to
do things not otherwise possible for us. I know it
is happening to me, and I know this is an even
greater gift than the beautiful sign I was so
blessed to receive.

Setting out on my first pilgrimage, I really
hoped for what someone called a "brush with the
supernatural." I was sure that if even one link of
my rosary chain turned to gold, I would know that
God really exists and my faith as a result would
become unshakeable. Yet, in the beautiful way
that Jesus and Mary know what we really need as
opposed to what we think we need, my experience in Medjugorje filled me with a trust in God
that I thought only a miraculous sign could instill.
By the time I left, I knew in my heart that God
does exist, that there is a heaven, that everything
the visionaries tell us Mary has been saying is
real, and that to know this I didn't need the sign I

thought I needed. Then, as a postscript, I got the sign.

I believe that I was meant to understand that, just as my broken crucifix was still valuable to me as it was, I didn't have to be perfect in order to be worthwhile. It turned out to be more than that: Mary is with us always, as she said. She is aware of even our smallest problems and when we try to give our hearts completely to Jesus, she obtains for us the grace and mercy that restores our brokenness to wholeness.

For whatever reason people go to Medjugorje, it changes them. If we then make the slightest effort to live out the change, the generosity of Jesus and Mary in helping us to draw closer to them cannot be equaled. The evidence of that in my own life is confirmed for me on a daily basis as I know it must be for you. I just read I John 4:13: *The way we know that He remains in us is from the Spirit that He gave us.*

I'm grateful that you issue such powerful ammunition for us foot soldiers in "Mary's Army." I hope our paths cross someday. My intention when my present tour of duty ends is to become a full-time member of Mary's Diplomatic Service, so it's natural that one of her "generals" and one of her "ambassadors" should meet sometime during the campaign.

Yours in the love
of Jesus and Mary,
Robert

Sweden

"Dear children, a heart which belongs to the Lord is splendid, even if it is flooded with difficulties and trials. But if the heart

engaged in difficulties strays away from God, it loses its splendor."—June 25, 1985

Dear Wayne,

I am writing you this letter because I feel I must. After reading your book on Medjugorje, I feel deeply touched and want to offer my services in any way I can to help others convert to Christ.

I really don't know where to start or how to begin, but I feel something inside that says go ahead and try. That's why I'm writing to you and asking for help in carrying the message to the young people of Medjugorje.

Until I got sober in the Fellowship of Alcoholics Anonymous ten years ago, my life was a total disaster. I was living in a hell of booze and drugs and could not see beyond the next drink or pill. Everyday, I would pray to God to lift this obsession only to find myself back into the old ways.

I had so much fear, self-hate, resentment, anger and loneliness inside of me that nothing seemed to take the pain away. Things seemed to be getting worse; I had to be high all of the time, for fear of the DT's coming back. What a life I was living—no friends, no job, no nothing. I was only 21, but had been using drugs and alcohol for seven years, and had made three appearances to the hospital detox wards in less than a six-month period.

I remember being strapped down in a hospital bed on Christmas day, realizing my life was almost over. Shortly after that, I was released from the hospital. I didn't have any booze in my body, but I had an overabundance of fear, hate and loneliness. And my body ached all over. I felt worse than I had ever felt in my life.

Then, a miracle happened. There's an old saying that goes something like when we are in our darkest moments or deepest despair, God hears our call and seems to lift us up on our feet again. I cried out that night in total despair, weeping and broken, saying, "God please take away this compulsion to drink and use drugs and I'll do anything You ask of me."

Well, that was 10 years ago and I have not had a drug or drink since. I have sponsored countless people, given hundreds of talks, and helped bring the simple message that everything will be all right if we trust God and clean house. I've sat calmly listening to others in some kind of crisis that I have felt the same way they did. We can bring all of our troubles into God's will for us.

I'm sorry for getting so far off the subject. Anyway, the main purpose of writing this letter is after reading in your book the heartbreak and struggle of Tanya's battle with drugs and peer pressure, and the young people there in Medjugorje migrating more and more to the bars and cafes, I would like to offer my services in helping them.

Maybe we could start a small group where we could share our strengths and experiences. Anyway, if it is possible for you to help me start such a group in Medjugorje, it would mean so much to me. I would pay for all my expenses, travel, food, room and board, etc. The only thing I ask for is a chance to continue to serve the Lord and carry His message.

Thank you very much,
Chris

Maryland

Dear Chris,

Thank you for your letter and commitment to want to help others who have suffered as you did. But I feel that you can contribute much more right there in your own community than you can at Medjugorje.

There is so much help needed among our own youth! Your example of overcoming your burdens through prayer and desire will assist many others. Our Lady visits Medjugorje daily and has many young people's prayer groups there. She will inspire, I am sure, converted souls in that area to help those in need.

Please know that I will pray for your commitment to penance for others. May Jesus and Mary always lead you.

In Christ,
Wayne

"It is going to be seven years soon that I have been coming to you. I ask you to renew in yourselves the messages I have given you. These are messages of prayer, peace, fasting, and penance. Make some penance yourselves. All of the other messages come from these four basic ones, but also live the other ones. Thank you for responding to my call. I am your Mother. Open your heart to the grace."—June 6, 1988

Marija Pavlovic is the visionary responsible for receiving the message on the 25th of each month that is relayed to the rest of the world. She has a keen sense of spiritual awareness. This young woman, whose life has been transformed, is visibly uneasy and shy with the crowds of pilgrims who gather outside of her small home several times a week.

Although she answers with enthusiasm the same

mundane questions endlessly repeated, she disdains requests for personal pictures and autographs. Privately she wonders why the pilgrims do not focus more on the spiritual instead of the phenomenal aspects of the apparitions.

Guarding her privacy far closer than the other visionaries, Marija prefers to spend more quiet time in prayer and occasionally in one-to-one conversation. She has a strong motherly love for those around her and is constantly doing things for visitors to her home. Of all the visionaries, she was the one who at the tender age of fifteen, long before the apparitions began, felt called to pursue a religious life.

In her role as a visionary in these ten years of grace from the Blessed Virgin, her commitment to living the messages as a personal example is readily apparent. I once asked her what happened in her daily apparitions, when she was not receiving the monthly message.

"The Blessed Mother prays with me for the petitions that I bring her from the pilgrims," she replied. "We pray especially for the very sick; in these visits we work, as She has asked in Her messages."

Marija sees her role as virtually living the messages— of prayer, fasting and penance. Especially penance: she is constantly going out of her way to help those most in need, including family.

Never was this more evident than in her tireless concern and work to save the life of her brother Andrija two years ago, when he was suffering from a terminal kidney disease. Andrija was 31, married with a three-year-old daughter, and working to support his family by taking in pilgrims.

As the disease worsened, and Andrija was no longer able to work, Marija grasped desperately at a spur-of-the-moment offer from a group of Americans for her to bring her dying brother to the United States for a kidney transplant operation. Against outcries from family members, she decided that she would be the donor for her brother.

In November, 1988, Marija and Andrija arrived at the University of Alabama at Birmingham Hospital, a renowned kidney disease center. Tests were conducted on both her and her brother over the next few weeks, and it was determined that Marija was a compatible donor for Andrija. The operation took place on December 16th; it was successful.

This loving act of penance saved Andrija's life—and changed it. For even though his sister was one of the visionaries, Andrija had not fully embraced the grace coming from the apparitions. His spiritual life, at best, lacked intensity. But when Marija volunteered to donate her kidney, he was overwhelmed.

It was not the sparing of his life that moved Andrija. It was the incredible act of love of one individual to another. Marija Pavlovic was—and is—living the messages.

Give some evidence that you mean to reform. Do not begin by saying to yourselves 'Abraham is our father.' I tell you, God can raise up children to Abraham from these stones. Even now the axe is laid to the root of the tree. Every tree that is not fruitful will be cut down and thrown into the fire. The crowds asked him, "What ought we to do?" In reply he said, "Let the man with two coats give to him who has none. The man who has food should do the same." [Luke 3:8-11]

6

The Great Sin of Our Time

"Where are the prayers which you used to address to me? My clothes were sparkling. Behold them soaked with tears. Oh, if you would know how the world today is plunged into sin. It seems to you that the world sins no longer, because here, you live in a peaceful world where there is neither confusion nor perversity."—November 6, 1983

We live in an age of indulgence. It is not like little Medjugorje, whose way of life is dictated by daily hard work, seasoned by a reverence for the things of God. Our indulgence derives from a modern-day philosophy that if a large part of society accepts or tolerates something that is against God's law, it's okay. Things like pre-marital sex. Or having babies out of wedlock. Or accepting homosexuality as a normal lifestyle. Fueled by our apathy, this philosophy allows and even encourages every commandment of God to be broken.

But in our time one such offense against God stands above the others: abortion. It looms over the entire world like a huge, flashing sign, giving a message of acceptance morally and legally of murder of the unborn.

This heinous sin, which has become a popular form

of birth-control, is total rejection of God's gift of life.

The wanton taking of life right from the mother's womb is more offensive than slavery or racial discrimination. It ranks with the genocidal slaughter of the concentration camps of World War II. The clean, sterile clinics used to proliferate this sin under the auspices of modern science and humanity, are more sophisticated but just as deadly effective as the death camps of the war. The number of victims is far greater. And the victims are not limited to one ethnic group.

The results however, are the same.

Of course, there are other great sins brought about by this modern philosophy: drugs, alcoholism, pornography, child abuse, family destruction through divorce—the list is painfully endless. But the abomination of abortion and its acceptance by people everywhere in the world graphically represents how far away mankind is from God. And it is strong evidence why the Mother of Jesus would call out to us for such an extended period of time, via the apparitions at Medjugorje to pray, fast, and do penance.

Abortion *is* indulgence in its ugliest interpretation; it *is* tolerated and encouraged. It *is* in complete opposition to every one of God's commandments. Its acceptance, legal as well as moral, is based on deception and lies.

God chose the womb of a woman as the most sacred dwelling place for Himself. It is His temple. The temple of the body for new life should be the most protected place on earth. It should be a place where life protects life. Yet, more than 60 million lives per year throughout the world are not allowed this protection. The mother's womb has become the modern battlefield. There are already more casualties on this battlefield than *all* of the wars in modern history.

The words of Jesus in Scripture underscore the cause of this horrible problem and put it in perspective; he said, (speaking of Satan) "Lying speech is his native tongue. He is a liar, and the father of lies."

For the father of lies, deceit and subtleties are the first step in hiding the truth completely. He veils it by calling the killing of the unborn "pro-choice." He convinces willing promoters of his evil to describe the early stages of newly-formed life as a "clump of cells." He deceives the victim mother into believing this is the best course for her and her future children. He uses high-profile personalities to lend their names and time to further the cause, calling it modern-day humanity to the poor, ignorant, and uneducated.

Thus, he builds his kingdom of death and uses his servants—the doctors, the nurses, the public relations firms, the media—to maintain it.

I always knew abortion was terribly wrong, even before learning and accepting the messages of the apparitions of Medjugorje. But I never actively did anything to stop it or protest against it. And even after the wonderful transformation we call conversion began in my life, I did little about it. My only contribution was to occasionally mention it in talks when speaking of sin. After all, Medjugorje was a message of love and peace. I didn't want to push anyone away from the message by getting into such controversial issues.

All that changed in May, 1989.

It was a hectic weekend. As I had done too many times in the past few years, I was scheduled to speak at two different locations on the same weekend. May being the month of Mary, I had eagerly accepted an invitation to speak at a small Marian conference in Virginia Beach, Virginia. Shortly after accepting, I received a call from planners of the first international conference on Medjugorje at Notre Dame, asking me to be among several guest speakers. It was scheduled for the weekend of May

12-13, the same dates as the event at Virginia Beach.

I called the conference planners in Virginia Beach to see if there was any way I could speak in the morning and leave early Saturday afternoon. They graciously complied, and I found myself booked at two diverse locations that would require a carefully-timed flight schedule in order to arrive at South Bend in time to speak on Saturday evening.

Arriving in Virginia Beach on Friday evening, I discovered the diversity of locations was not the only comparison of the two Marian conferences. There were only about 70 people in attendance; Notre Dame was expecting 7,000 or more. Virginia Beach was informal and had only three speakers; Notre Dame had a full schedule of nine speakers and other activities.

That evening, we were to discuss informally the various aspects of Marian apparitions. Somehow the subject of abortion came up early, and the rest of the evening was devoted to it. It created an uneasiness within me, as I had recently felt convicted by the Holy Spirit to do more than just casually mention the sin of abortion in my talks.

That Friday evening session seemed to be a confirmation that I was to begin—this weekend—speaking out about this controversial issue. And the next morning I began.

For the first time, I spoke about abortion being part of the message of Medjugorje; we were to "get our hands dirty" I told the small audience, to become involved in living the messages by applying them to urgent needs in our society and our daily lives. Only in this way could we rid our community, country and world of such sins that had become accepted through modern-age philosophy of anything goes. I spoke with deep feeling for nearly two hours. It felt wonderful.

I left just before noon, and three plane transfers later, I arrived exhausted, disheveled—but very happy, in South

Bend for the Notre Dame Conference.

Entering the Convocation Center, I had less than an hour before speaking, and only fifteen minutes allotted time, as I was a last-minute addition to the guest roster. Still charged from the morning's session, I wondered how I could possibly get the same fervent message which had taken two hours that morning across to the 7,000 assembled at Notre Dame.

Somehow, it happened. I went to bed that evening a little after midnight, completely spent but filled with a new sense of mission.

That Sunday May morning was very special; it was Mother's Day; it was also the anniversary of the beginning of the 1917 Fatima apparitions of Our Lady; and to top it off, it was Pentecost Sunday. I awoke in a twilight that was still more sleep than awake.

As I lay in bed, mentally praying a short prayer to the Holy Spirit to begin my day, I suddenly had the most beautiful vision—or dream; whichever it was, it was vivid and clear. I saw the hand of Mary, and in it was a small, translucent embryo hand; She gently brought it forward, toward me. No words were spoken in the vision; they were not necessary. The vision was final, total confirmation for me that I was to speak out about the evil of abortion and make known that its eradication through prayer, fasting and penance was definitely a part and purpose of the Medjugorje message.

I could hardly wait for the next speaking engagement, in Los Angeles, the following weekend.

That first night in a jammed church located in a Hispanic section of Los Angeles, I began as never before, jumping immediately in the first few minutes to the horror of abortion. It was probably too much too soon but I couldn't help it. The vision of that little hand extended to me by the Blessed Virgin Mary was burned into my mind. People squirmed. And then something happened that had never happened before in four years of ministry: several people near the back got up and walked out. I felt my heart jump, but I continued and eventually got around to speaking about the love and peace of the Medjugorje message.

Afterwards, as the people came to the front of the huge Spanish church to greet me, many made clear that they were uneasy by the message, but several added that they felt it was necessary that we see all sides to the call to live the messages.

As the crowd began to diminish there was a young woman left standing in front of me. She was visibly shaken and was trembling as she approached me, looking all around to be sure no one was within hearing distance. Then in a quavering voice, tears streaming down her cheeks she asked me, "Do you think that God will forgive a mother who had an abortion, and didn't know any better at the time?"

I knew that she was the mother and that it had taken great courage to come forth and ask such a revealing question. I also knew that this was deliverance from the darkness of guilt she had borne since her abortion. I understood what Mother Teresa had meant when she was quoted as saying that there are two deaths in the sin of abortion—that of the unborn, and the conscience of the mother.

I took her by the hands to quiet the trembling and now sobbing girl. "Yes," I said softly, "A thousand times yes. He forgives when we come forward and repent. Find a priest, or pastor (I didn't ask her what faith she was) and talk to him." I then gave her a medal from Medjugorje and hugged her. She staggered as she left, hardly able to walk under the tremendous emotional release of God's forgiving love.

There were more such traumatic incidents in the following weeks. And I vowed never to let up, until the horrible sin of abortion was completely eradicated from the face of this earth.

"You know that I love you and am coming here out of love, so I could show you the path of peace and salvation for your souls. I want you to listen to me and not permit Satan to seduce you. Dear children, Satan is strong enough! Therefore, I ask you to dedicate your prayers so that those who are under his influence may be saved. Give witness by your life; sacrifice your lives for the salvation of the world.—February 25, 1988

Here's a letter I received from a mother in Georgia. It's long, but this one I feel I must share in its entirety. Because the courage of this woman, whose name I have changed, may be just the encouragement another woman might need to make a similar decision. I was in tears before I finished it; perhaps you will be, too.

Dear Wayne,

I have wanted to go to Medjugorje ever since I saw you on the Sally Jessy Raphael Show in February, 1987. The message (of Medjugorje) and your experience there was personal for me because things were happening in my life (at that time) which I couldn't explain. Yet, when I watched the show, I realized these things weren't just happening to me!

I cried until noon that day. I was so touched that I called the show and was given your address. I then sat and wrote you a letter, but I never mailed it, because I thought you might think I was crazy. Now, almost four years later I still have the letter and would like to share with you what was in it.

In March of 1985, I made a Cursillo retreat, which was to be an encounter with Jesus. I didn't have a relationship with the Lord—I only knew Him as the Creator. I was Catholic, having been baptized as an infant and received the sacraments, thus fulfilling the "obligation" of my parents. My mother is Catholic but she never openly prayed or taught us children how to pray. She never even spoke of God except to blame Him for her sufferings. My father was Lutheran and of the two, he had, and expressed, his faith.

So it was in my background not to be religious. At the time I made Cursillo, I was married with three teenage children. In fact, I was going only to please my husband who had made the weekend two weeks before. He was not a religious man, but somehow he had changed. I was curious enough to go and find out what had changed him. He was full of love, joy, and peace. All he talked about was Jesus.

Well, on my weekend everyone was finding Jesus except me. The night before the retreat was over, we all went into the chapel to pray. It was there that I felt a presence, yet I knew it was not Jesus. It was a motherly presence and it wasn't until someone began to pray the litany of Mary that I realized I felt "her" presence. There was a knowing in my heart that Jesus had sent her to me and that through her I would come to Him. At the close of the weekend, everyone shared how they found Jesus. I got up and shared how I found the Blessed Mother.

And so began the "message." Within a few days

I began having the same dream at least once a week. I kept dreaming of a cross made from tree branches on a hill with rocks everywhere. I was troubled by the dream, thinking it meant someone I loved was going to die. The dream continued for two years, and then I saw the vision (of the dream, with the cross on the hill) on the video of Medjugorje that was shown on the Sally Jessy Raphael Show.

In May of the same year, (two months later) I became pregnant. My youngest child was thirteen. This pregnancy, unlike my others was going to be painfully different.

I continually bled from the beginning and later was hospitalized. The doctors tried to convince me that I was having a miscarriage, and that I needed to abort the baby. The doctor taking care of me was a friend of my family doctor, and in the hospital was the first time I had ever met him. He and his associates, some friends and even some family members tried to convince my husband and me that abortion was the answer. They told me I would never carry full term. I was 36, and my age was against me. I would only suffer and make my family suffer and that the child probably would not be born healthy.

But all I could think of later when they did a sonogram, was this tiny little heart beating. In my heart I then heard, "This child is a gift of God." Well, I left the hospital still bleeding and in pain. I was told to call and make an appointment with the doctor in four days, as he was sure I would have lost the child by that time.

I suffered for those days. Then, I called for an appointment, but I had lost the doctor's number so I called information. What I didn't realize was, I was given the number of a different doctor.

When I arrived the next day with my husband, the receptionist told me she had no record of my hospital stay or that the doctor had ever seen me. However, she saw that I was in pain so she took me right in to see this doctor. He was kind, understanding, compassionate—and Catholic! He shared his faith and gave me encouragement. I left his office and was told to stay off my feet completely, and so I did for the next two months.

Still in pain and still bleeding, I spent that time praying from my heart. I knew that the Blessed Mother was with me. Then, in early September, I awoke at three in the morning with hard contractions and I was hemorrhaging heavily. I crawled into the bathroom, crying in pain, and didn't even have the strength to call out to my husband who was downstairs watching TV. I prayed to the Blessed Mother, begging Her to help my child.

Suddenly, I was surrounded by a bright white mist going around me and through me. I could not see beyond the light. I was instantly praying the "Our Father," yet it was not just me praying— I heard others praying with me. I was filled with peace and had no pain.

The next morning, I awoke and I had stopped bleeding, and there was no pain! In March, 1986, I gave birth to a beautiful, healthy baby girl. When I looked at her, I saw the eyes of the Blessed Mother. Unlike my other children, this baby had beautiful blue eyes and her hair a dark brown. She is truly a gift of God.

What happened that night changed my life

beyond words. The Blessed Mother led me directly to Jesus, and Jesus gave this baby to me.

After all this time, I still have not gone to Medjugorje, but the message keeps coming to me. I feel like I've been there a thousand times.

> In the Hearts of Jesus
> and Mary,
> Judy

Georgia

"Dear children, I am calling you to complete surrender to God. Pray, little children, that Satan does not sway you like branches in the wind. Be strong in God. I desire that through you the whole world may get to know the God of Joy. Neither be anxious nor worried. God will help you and show you the way. I want you to love all men with my love, both the good and the bad. . ." —May 25, 1988

Dear Mr. Weible,

I recently had the opportunity to hear you speak at (our church, Oct. '90) in New Jersey. I was invited to go by my mother and her husband who have recently been to Medjugorje. I was raised Catholic but have been struggling with my faith for about eight years now. I am 32 years old. I have always believed in Jesus Christ, but was never quite ready or willing or able (or all three) to really know and live in Jesus.

So, here I am, listening to you speak and really loving every word I heard. And then, you began to speak about abortion. I had one about ten years ago, knowing fully what I was doing, but seeing no other solution at the time. I confessed this sin only last year, having not been to confession in fifteen years.

All of this sounds so matter-of-fact, doesn't it? And that's exactly how I felt for ten years. Then, you spoke about a young girl, nervous, tearful and afraid, who asked you if God could forgive a mother—I choked back the tears, but they came anyway. I remember wishing that my mother wasn't sitting next to me to see me, because "she would know." In those very moments, I don't know if my eyes were open or closed, (but) I saw the face of a young boy about ten years old, and I heard a voice in my mind say, "He is with Me."

I stopped crying and continued to listen. It wasn't until later that evening that I thought about the vision and the voice and actually comprehended and believed that Jesus was telling me directly that I will see my son someday. I was very excited about this and could hardly believe that this could happen to me.

This evening, I was reading the Bible, and while reading a word-study for the words *grace* and *mercy*, I came upon this quote by the German scholar, Bengel: "Grace takes away the guilt; mercy (takes away) the misery." It has all finally come together for me. That evening as I listened to you, I experienced the grace and mercy of our Lord Jesus Christ, and it has led me to peace. I never want to be without it again.

Thanks for saying yes when She called.

Love, from a sister in Christ,
Lori

New Jersey

It was a beautiful Catholic church located in one of the suburbs of St Louis. This evening, it was packed. Medjugorje fever was strong in this community, and I was happy to be here to speak about the Blessed Mother's apparitions at Medjugorje for the second time in the past two years. But this night, somewhere in the talk, I would speak about abortion. About half-way into the program, it came—unplanned, as always, and as everything else in my talks.

Less than two minutes into explaining why I thought abortion and other evils that had so captured our society were part of the reasons that Our Lady continually pleaded with us to pray and fast, two Catholic nuns in full habit got up in protest and walked out.

I sighed and carried on. The father of lies and deceit, in his quest to convince God's children to reject His precious gift of life, had done his work well .

Filled with a deep sadness that even the religious could be persuaded by Satan's lies, I silently renewed my vow to continue to speak out against abortion at every Medjugorje talk. A little while later, as if by way of confirmation, I got this letter:

Dear Wayne,

Today, I played a tape a friend loaned to me of your talk last night at our church. Part of your talk was about Mary's hand cradling a hand of a baby. I know Mary must want you to soften people's hearts with your words. Abortion is hurting all of us.

When I was 18, I ran away to college to escape my home life filled with alcoholism. Caught up in fear and confusion (and having left my faith) I had an abortion my freshman year.

Ten years later, through God's love, I returned

to my faith and slowly back to my church. At this time I now had a daughter four years of age. The memory of what I had done was causing me overwhelming guilt. I was afraid to go to confession because of the innocent death I had caused.

Finally, a year later, I did go to confession. The elderly priest I confessed my abortion to I know now surely was our Lord speaking to my heart what I longed to hear. Father looked into my eyes and said, "Your sin is forgiven; now don't be so hard on yourself."

I thought that was that. Now it was over. Well, a good three or four years later, I was puttering around the house on my day off. I looked outside at the beautiful day and something in my mind said to go visit "Holy Hill" Shrine. As you may know, that is a shrine to our Blessed Lady outside of Milwaukee, where people have been healed.

Anyway, I went. Before leaving (the shrine), I stopped in the religious book store there where a 25-cent Catholic pamphlet kept catching my eye. It was prayers and steps of healing for miscarried and aborted children. I thought of my sister (who has had miscarriages), and that maybe (Blessed Virgin) Mary wants me to give this to her.

When I was home alone a few days later, I read it and realized Mary had another step for me to take. I then prayed to know the sex of my aborted child. A boy. I named him John, after John the Baptizer. I prayed next, as the pamphlet said, to have Mary and Jesus baptize my baby and give him all the love I had not. I prayed for the abortion physician whose soul is so in need of saving; for the nurses involved that day; and, for the father who had rejected our baby, as well.

Next, I had a mass said for my baby. By "coincidence," the Scripture reading was on John the Baptizer.

The following year, on Mother's Day, I was saying my prayers, and it struck me that I was praying the Hail Mary too fast. With that, I began to pray it slowly, thinking about the words and what they mean, when I heard a little voice break through and say, "Mom, I want to say, I love you."

Two or three years later, I was able to go to Medjugorje for the Feast of the Assumption, to thank Our Lady for loving me. My last night in Medjugorje, I climbed Mt. Krizevac. Up there I again was saying my Hail Mary when I was stopped by (the words) "Pray for us now and at the hour of our death." I realized how very proud we should be that Mary, the mother of Jesus, prays for *us* now and that She also prays for us as we are dying.

Please don't feel bad if some are unhappy to hear your words on abortion. Some are slower in seeing the truth. I know, because I was one of them.

God bless you and your family,
Patricia

Wisconsin

"Prepare your hearts for these days when the Lord particularly desires to purify you from all the sins of your past. . ."—December 4, 1986

It had been a good evening. The theater in this Philadelphia suburb was jammed to the last seat, with many people having to stand in the back. The message of Medjugorje resounded positively, with emotion and impact in the hearts of those in attendance—except for a few.

Several women had abruptly left at the mention of abortion. Afterwards, as I made my way toward the back of the theater, one young woman waited nervously for an opportunity to speak to me. She planted herself determinedly in front of me. I knew immediately she was not there to thank me for the evening's program. "I just want to ask you one question," she said with unhidden anger, "Why did you have to talk about abortion? I thought this was to be a talk about the apparitions of the Blessed Mother at Medjugorje. It's supposed to be a message of peace and—"

"It is, it is," I interrupted, "but it's also about how we live and —"

"That's all well and good, but I brought a special friend I've been trying for months to convince this is real. Everything was going fine—then she left when you started on abortion. Now, what am I supposed to say to her?" She abruptly turned and left, too upset to wait for my response.

It wasn't the first time I had been challenged for including the sins of this generation in my talks, nor would it be the last. But the good fruits that came from it dictated that it must continue to be part of the message.

I recalled the smartly-dressed young woman in Seattle, who approached me, outside of the church where I had been speaking. Tears had streaked her carefully made-up face. "I want you to know I came today as a woman who believes in our rights, and in full support of the pro-choice movement; I leave here a firm believer in Medjugorje—and very much pro-life. God bless you!"

There are other examples good and bad: broken parents asking for prayers for their 14-year-old daughter who had just undergone an abortion in a state that does not require parental consent; a young teenage couple, contritely, but with courage confessing *their dual responsibility* in choosing abortion, and now seeking spiritual guidance; a young Australian woman breaking down in uncontrolled sobs, sitting in the middle of a packed auditorium.

There are no quick and easy solutions that will bring about the eradication of abortion and other great sins of our time. Legislation in itself won't accomplish it; morals cannot be legislated. Society has to support laws willingly, with the inherent goodness and free will God gives to every individual.

The obvious solution for those who believe is to follow the requests of Our Lady. She asks us to pray and to fast; put prayer and fasting together and ask specifically each day for an end to this and other offenses against God. Do it with confidence and trust.

In Ramah is heard the sound of moaning, of bitter weeping! Rachel mourns her children, she refuses to be consoled because her children are no more. [Jer. 31:15]

7

"Let it unfold as a flower for God..."

"Tonight especially I would like to invite all the parents in the world to find time for their children and family. May they offer love to their children. May this love that they offer be parental and motherly love. Once again, dear children, I call you to family prayer. During one of the previous encounters your Mother asked you to renew the family prayer. I ask that again tonight."—July 31, 1989

One of the most memorable messages given by the Blessed Virgin Mary came on Podbrdo, the Hill of Apparitions, on a Monday during my first trip to Medjugorje. It has remained for me the single most important part of the spiritual equation that leads to the peace and happiness promised by living the messages.

Similar to the message above, it called us to utilize the strongest spiritual medicine possible: family prayer. It asked us to begin our witness and our work for God within the family where the need for conversion is the strongest.

We arrived in Medjugorje on that first trip on Friday afternoon. The first three days of pilgrimage became a blur of attending Mass, climbing hills and being an active part of the huge "family" of pilgrims present there during that week. I had never spent so much time in church. And I liked it! I felt a true sense of family closeness to my fellow pilgrims and to the Croatian villagers.

By Monday, I yearned only to be a permanent part of all this; the so-called real world was very far away and its daily needs were all but forgotten. I didn't eat or sleep much. I just wanted this warm, spiritual togetherness to go on forever.

That evening as we gathered for dinner at our hotel in Citluk, we were suddenly interrupted by our guide with startling news: during the evening's usual apparition Our Lady stated that she would appear again that night on Podbrdo, for a special apparition. This was the hill where She had first appeared to the visionaries. And we were invited to be there.

Forgetting about the meal, we dashed for the waiting bus outside of the hotel. When we arrived at the hill, I was a little disappointed; there were so many people there! For some reason, I thought this was just for our group. But as we joined the stream of pilgrims climbing the hill in solid darkness, groping our way up the steep, rocky path, I quickly realized that it was a real blessing just to be part of all of this. Upon reaching the top I realized that Mary had called her "family" together for this special gift. There were thousands present! The quiet murmur of united prayer swelled in reverent response to a holy moment of time.

She came around eleven o'clock. After what seemed like hours of waiting in the dark, the precious happening was over in a matter of minutes.

But the message, given shortly after the visionaries gave the soft exclamation of "Ode" (which means "she's gone" in Croatian), would never be forgotten by me. It would become the anchor message of my mission to take the messages of Medjugorje to families all over the world. In that unique gathering that made us all feel like brothers and sisters, the mother of Jesus gently asked us to go home from our pilgrimage and to pray together as a family. She said if we would pray together, then we would grow holy together, adding, *"And then I can present your family as a beautiful flower that unfolds for my Son, Jesus."*

That "beautiful flower" was crushed in my first marriage by a traumatic divorce. It was an ugly, hate-filled divorce, full of accusation and court-room drama; it created terrible scars on the four children that were a product of that broken family.

When Mary Virgin spoke to my heart on that fateful evening in October of 1981, she called me her son. It made me feel for the first time in my life that Jesus was a real, flesh-and-blood God. By my acceptance, I became an active member of the Holy Family, a membership open to all people of the world. And, the first ones I desired to recruit and convince that what was happening to me was real were my four older children.

In the ensuing months I met solid resistance to my efforts on behalf of this new way of conversion from Lisa, Steve, Angela and Michael, who were by then very much of the world.

And why not? The family had become geographically and emotionally divided. Later, I had remarried, and so had their mother. There was no nucleus—no family prayer, no family sharing, no family anything. My former wife and I seemed to be always pulling at their emotions and loyalties, creating constant tension. They had drifted off into their own little space, their own little world. It was a world without the love of family togetherness so vital to children.

As far as they were concerned, their father had "flipped out" and had become a religious fanatic. They didn't really believe that the mother of Jesus had actually spoken to me. Long, pleading monologues were met with stoney stares, or eyes rolled to heaven in the hope it would mercifully end soon. In our sporadic visits, I would bring the subject up often; just as often, they would make a hasty retreat, citing some task that needed to be done at that very moment. My heart was broken.

Finally one evening while commiserating my frustrations to Terri, she once again displayed that wonderful gift of discernment that most wives seem to receive. She told me with gentle resolve that I would be better off *living* the messages and letting my children see the results, rather than battering them with marathon lectures about what had happened to me. It was difficult to accomplish in fact, but turned out to be very wise advice.

One evening, after more than a year of traveling the world to witness about the messages of Medjugorje, the telephone rang. It was my oldest daughter, Lisa. She had heard that I would be speaking right here in South Carolina, in Spartanburg. In a somewhat condescending tone, Lisa told me, "Dad, Angela and I are thinking we might drive to Spartanburg to hear you speak." She let that register with me before adding, "We figured it wouldn't hurt us to at least listen, since it's so close."

I was thrilled, but I didn't want to let her know, so I said, "That's great. It'll give us some time to together."

I drove to Spartanburg filled with all kinds of thoughts. I had prayed hard for the conversion of my four children who had been so hurt by the divorce. Was this just to appease their father—or were they seriously interested at last?

It was a wonderful evening. The auditorium was filled with a good mix of Catholics and non-Catholics. After all, this was the heart of the Bible Belt, a stronghold of Southern Baptists. I may have spoken with added intensity, hoping my daughters would feel and see the effects such a wonderful miracle was having.

Afterwards, people came rushing up to the podium. It was a good witness, and many were deeply moved. I looked for Lisa and Angela, and then spotted them in the rear of the auditorium. Lisa was sobbing uncontrollably in Angela's arms. Angie looked at me and turned her free hand up in a gesture indicating to me that she didn't know what was wrong with her older sister.

It took awhile to make my way through the crowd and reach my children. Lisa had finally stopped crying—until she saw me. Falling into my arms, she started all over again. A few moments later with her arms around my neck, through her tears she said softly, "Daddy, that wasn't you speaking; that was God. I really believe that, and I want to go to Medjugorje."

Then I fought back tears.

Several months later, Lisa did go to Medjugorje. She came home and began enthusiastically witnessing to the rest of the family—meeting much the same resistance I had. Shortly, Angela wanted to know more about it and was soon attending a small Baptist church near her home with her husband, Roy.

The beautiful flower which I feared had been crushed, was beginning to open.

"Dear children, tonight I wish to tell you during the days of this novena to pray for the outpouring of the Holy Spirit on your families and on your parish. Pray, and you shall not regret it. God will give you gifts by which you will glorify Him till the end of your life on this earth."—June 2, 1984

Dear Wayne,

First of all I'd like to thank you from my heart for what you have done for me and my family. It all started with the newsletter (Miracle at Medjugorje), part one. After reading that the Blessed Virgin Mary was appearing to six children, something really moved in my heart. Something inside of me wanted to go to Medjugorje.

My wife and I were married in an Anglican church. Nothing much is said about the Virgin Mary in our parish. I was Catholic before I married. We sent our children to a Catholic school, because we knew that we couldn't teach them religion at home.

This desire inside of me to go to Medjugorje grew deeper and deeper until finally we decided to go. Our whole family went in April, 1989. I won't go into detail about all of the things that happened to us there, but I have to mention one that totally changed our lives.

We climbed Apparition Hill (Podbrdo) with our group and for some reason, my camera acted funny; it went on taking pictures like I would never run out of film. The film was 36 exposure but the number on the camera ended at seventy-seven. One of our group said he thought something was wrong with the camera.

Before the rosary hour at six that evening, we had some free time. My family and I decided to go back up the hill. We wanted to take some more pictures, (thinking) it would be a shame to go home without any pictures if the previous film did not turn out.

After being on Apparition Hill for about an hour in meditation and prayer, it was time to go

back for the rosary hour. On the way down, something inspired me to take my shoes off and walk
down barefoot. I got down okay, with no scratches
or bruises on my feet. I was looking for a place to
put my shoes on and there really was no place to
sit down. A few feet away there was a gravel pile
with a plank over it. I climbed on top and sat
down and, as I looked down onto the gravel in
front of my feet, I saw a little cross. I bent down to
pick it up and I couldn't believe my eyes. It was a
beautiful black rosary.

That morning before the service, we had
bought some rosaries to bring home as souvenirs.
I had no intention of using them other than as a
remembrance of Medjugorje. I didn't know what
to do with the rosary I had found. I wanted to
give it back to whoever lost it. I had asked around
but no one claimed it. I asked Father John, who
was our leader and he said for me to keep it, as it
was meant for me.

We came home Friday afternoon very tired. We
had company that evening that wanted to know
all about the trip. Saturday, we were still trying to
recover from it all and we decided to go to bed
early. But something inside of me asked the family to pray the rosary. I couldn't believe my eyes
and ears when they all came with no questions
asked. It was the first time in our lives that we
prayed the rosary together as a family. I know that
no one could have led us to pray like that but the
holy mother of God.

Since that day our lives have started to change.
The children are a lot calmer. They don't fight
like they used to and there's more love, peace and
unity like never before. My oldest daughter came

to me and said, "Dad, you have changed!" I asked
her how. She said, "You don't yell as much as you
did before." I told her there was no reason to yell
anymore, there was no more fighting. From that
day on I have prayed the rosary everyday. The
family prays it together as often as we can.

> Yours in Christ,
> Bill, and family

Saskatchewan, Canada

*"Dear children, you are on Tabor. You receive blessings, strength
and love. Carry them into your families and into your homes.
To each one of you, I grant a special blessing. Continue in
joy, prayer and reconciliation."—June 24, 1986*

Dear Wayne and Terri,

Having recently read your book Wayne, and
viewed a video on Medjugorje, I wanted to write
and say how much I have enjoyed it all. I have
longed to go to Medjugorje, but if I never get
there, I will feel I have been there through these
items.

Before I was married 17 years ago, we always
said the family rosary in our home as my mother
had a great devotion to Our Lady. But when I
married, my husband was not a "rosary" man and
I was lucky if I could get him to say three Hail
Marys with us at prayer time. I always said a
decade with my daughters. The suggestion of the
whole rosary would have caused them to rebel, so
I was pleased they were happy to say even a
decade.

However, when my husband saw the video of you and Leon LeGrand (of Australia; a businessman with a similar conversion experience), he was very taken with the experiences of both of you and the messages of Medjugorje.

Then, one night in September last year (1990), a very horrible film called "Catholic Boys" was shown on TV. It was blasphemous and most disrespectful. This made my husband Jack very angry. He tried to have it stopped by getting as many people as possible to ring the station and object, as the previews of the movie were shown for several days in advance. I suggested we pray the rosary to see if that would help. Well, it certainly did but not in the way we intended.

The movie was shown, but a big rugby match was on at the same time on another station and asking around for a few days later, we found only one person who actually watched the film. But the next night Jack said, "Right! From now on we are saying the family rosary!"

Even though one daughter asked if he meant every night, they came happily to join us without any fuss. Had it been my suggestion, there would be an outcry, but because their father suggested it, they didn't object.

I doubt you have time to even read the mail you must get, and knowing how busy you are, I don't expect a reply to this. Maybe you could say a little prayer for our family. I shall in return say one for the Weible family.

Keep up the good work—both of you.

With love and prayers,
Carmel

Australia

"Each Thursday read again the passage of Matthew 6:24-34, before the Most Blessed Sacrament; or, if it is not possible to come to church, do it with your family."—March 5, 1984

Dear Wayne,

I had to sit down and write you this letter. I have just finished reading your book and quite frankly, I don't know when I've ever been so moved.

I have always had a great faith in Our Lady. I have a son who just turned 18 years old. When he was born, we were told he shouldn't live a year. He was born with an imperforated anus, one kidney, bladder reflux and a severe scoliosis of the spine.

Well, one by one each of his "problems" was remedied and he did outlive that one year! This, in itself is a miracle. Truly, the only way I was able to keep any strength through all of his operations and hospital stays was my faith in Our Blessed Lady and Her Son, Jesus.

Things went along well until May, 1990. He was hospitalized in respiratory failure and was very sick. We were told that due to the severity of his scoliosis and the fact that he was growing, he had what is called restrictive lung disease. This was a real curve. I thought all the hurt and worries were behind us.

Anyway during all of this turmoil, I've been reading your book and praying harder than ever to my best friend, Our Lady. A couple of weeks ago when I was feeling particularly down, she

gave me a beautiful gift—she turned my rosary to
gold! I am thrilled with that wonderful sign. I am,
however, so very tense about Michael. He is such
a good boy. I also have a lovely daughter who has
suffered in her own fashion due to her brother's
problems.

I sometimes feel that my prayers are not being
heard. When I felt that way, I would read a passage or chapter in your book. I guess what I am
trying to say through all this rambling is that your
book has kept me going.

I am praying for a miracle for Michael. I'd like
to see him lead a normal life, graduate in June
and go on to college without any other worries. I
ask you to pray for him and we will pray for you.

God bless you, Wayne,
Anita

New Jersey

*"Dear children, tonight your Mother would like to call you,
like I have done before, to renew prayer in the families. Dear
children, the family needs to pray today. I wish, dear children,
that you would renew again my messages through this prayer."—
February 2, 1990*

Dear Mr. Weible,

I can't begin to tell you what your newsletter
has meant to me. Although my husband is a non-
Christian, I am Catholic and your newsletter has
been a factor in deepening my faith.

In attempting to answer the call of Our Blessed
Mother to prayer and conversion, I have been

blessed with the ability to understand more fully God's workings in my life. I have also started on a path of becoming a witness, rather than a nag to my husband, and my hopes for his eventual conversion have become just that—hopes instead of anxieties.

Prayer has become as necessary to me as food, and although I am sadly negligent about praying the rosary, I do take time every day to be alone with God. By meeting with Him daily, I am beginning to understand what it means to be a friend of Christ; it is nothing less than astounding.

Although I have been through and am still going through some periods of heavy chastisement, I am learning to accept even these with joy, understanding that God truly does love those He corrects. All of the prayers, rituals, etc., that I learned growing up Catholic and that had become somewhat stagnant for me have taken on new meaning and new life. My soul sings with the knowledge of the manifestations of the Risen Lord's love in my life!

Yours in the Risen Christ,
Patricia

Massachusetts

How happy I was when my oldest daughter Lisa, came and listened to one of my talks, converted, and then went to Medjugorje. She influenced the other three children of my previous marriage by her example. When they visited with us in Myrtle Beach, we prayed a family rosary together—even though they were all of the Baptist faith.

Even my oldest son, Steve, joined us in body, if not in spirit. He was the only one still resisting. Angie and her little family were attending church each Sunday; even Michael had asked to learn to pray the rosary and seemed to enjoy going to church with us. What was more, they seem blessed by it. And of course, I was inwardly delighted that we were fulfilling the Blessed mother's appeal: *"Keep on praying that My plans be completely realized. I request the families of the parish to pray the Family Rosary."*—*October 4, 1984*

But not Steve. He had always been my "thorn." Always in mucky little trouble, he seemed unable to conform to society. To make matters worse, I had been forced to go to court, to accomplish his earnest plea to come live with me. It only created more hatred and for him, estrangement from his mother. She saw it as his deserting her.

Even now, with the wonderful changes taking place in the others, nothing had really changed for Steve. He couldn't seem to keep a job, or get along with others, including his brother and sisters. After enlisting for six years in the Air Force, Steve had returned home after only two years from his assignment in the Philippines. He was discharged early for not being able to get along in military life. His life continued to amount to a big, fat zero.

After one particularly memorable confrontation with Steve, I remembered the story of Victor Wee, from Singapore; I remembered how he had prayed and fasted for his atheist mother to convert to Christianity before her death. That night, I pleaded in prayer for a solution to the problem of my son, vowing to renew my efforts to pray and to fast for his conversion.

Immediately my heart was filled with an unexpected message: *Send him to school.*

What? Could the Blessed Mother possibly be asking me to waste my time and money again by placing him in school? This young thorn in my side who had barely graduated from high school? But the message remained clearly: *Send him to school.*

Terri laughed when I told her what had happened. "Go ahead and waste your money!" she said. And that's exactly what I thought I would be doing. But, if that was what Our Lady wanted. . .

I traveled to Columbia, South Carolina where Steve and my other children were living. After the usual lecture in which I expressed for the thousandth time how he had disappointed me in just about everything, I sat him down and told him to listen carefully, because this was his last chance

"Steve, I don't know why I'm doing this," I began, knowing in my heart he would only last at best a short semester of summer school, "but—I'm going to pay for you to attend the University of South Carolina. I'm going to pay for tuition and books, but you have to get a steady job and pay for your room and board. And I'm not going to do any of the legwork for enrollment; that's up to you. If you don't do it, you won't go."

There was complete surprise and shock in his face. I continued: "If you make below a C grade, then I don't pay, and if you flunk out, the deal's over!"

Suddenly my son reached over and hugged me, exclaiming, "Dad, I love you; and I can't believe you're really doing this!"

I thought to myself, "Neither can I!"

Changes began to be seen almost immediately. Steve's entire demeanor altered. He took care of all the necessary tasks to enroll at the university; he started to get along with everyone; he even got a job.

The greatest change, though, took place with his mother. On Mother's Day, Steve went by his mother's house, as he always did for holidays. Visits with his mother usually were short; they were always strained with stiff, formal politeness prevalent whenever disagreement or smouldering problems within families were left unresolved. She had never really confronted the problem with Steve. She never wanted to talk about it. He had made attempts to no avail, and of course, that was a major part of the problem.

Steve was startled when finally on this Mother's Day, she began talking about the divorce and his desertion of her. As she broke into tears, Steve jumped at the chance he had been waiting for, for more than ten years. "Mom," he said, kneeling in front of her and looking right at her, "It's time we talked about this and got it past us."

"Oh, no—you're not going to ruin my day!" she shot back. Lisa, who had arrived with Steve, backed Steve and told her mother it was time they settled it once and for all. Their mother had no choice but to listen.

Two hours later, after much yelling, crying and accusing (with mediation by Lisa), their mother began to weep uncontrollably. Steve knelt down again and taking his mother by the hand said, "Momma, this has been between us far too long; Mom—I love you! Can't we just put this behind us and start over?"

She looked at him and then hugged him saying, "I love you! We can try!"

A mother found her son—and the son, a mother.

I went to Columbia shortly after this and while driving Steve to the university for his enrollment, he told me what had happened on Mother's Day. I began to cry; I knew it was the beginning of his conversion. It was a proud day for me to see my "thorn" finally attending the school from which his father had graduated. Even if it only lasted a summer semester, the fruit was already evident.

Steve lasted more than the first one-course semester. He managed to make the grade of B+ on his first course, —a miracle of its own. And he has continued to carry a B average. Best of all, beyond what I dared hope, Steve—

no longer a thorn in his father's side—is regularly attending church.

The last petals of the beautiful flower have unfolded, and Our Lady is now able to present it to Jesus in full bloom!

"You who are wives, be submissive to your husbands. This is your duty in the Lord. Husbands, love your wives. Avoid any bitterness toward them. You children, obey your parents in everything as the acceptable way in the Lord. And fathers, do not nag your children lest they lose heart." [Col. 3:18- 21]

8

Youth: "Send them to Me..."

"Tonight your Mother is happy, happy, happy to be with you and to see you in such large numbers. I am happy for what we have done in this Year of the Youth. We have stepped a step forward. I would like to see in the future, parents in the families work and pray as much as they can with their children, so they can, from day to day, strengthen their spirit. Your Mother is here to help each one of you. Open yourselves to your Mother; She is waiting for you. May this moment you will live at midnight be a moment of thanksgiving for everything you received during this year."—August 14, 1989, on the eve of the Feast of the Assumption, on the Hill of Apparitions to thousands of youth.

It was a unique and special occasion the evening the above message from Mary was received by the visionaries on the Hill of Apparitions; they said they had never seen Our Lady so happy.

Thousands of young people filled every inch of holy ground around the spot where Gospa had first appeared. The evening marked the high point of the first organized youth festival in Medjugorje. It was a festival She had personally requested on the Feast of the Assumption the previous year, calling for the coming year to be known as the Year of the Youth. The festival has occurred every year since with tens of thousands of young people in attendance under the mantle of the Blessed Mother for a week of prayer and sharing.

It is no accident that Our Lady chose six youths to appear to at this remote site in Yugoslavia. There was nothing really special about them other than they were young, and like most youths, their hearts were open and ready. Among the six, only Marija had expressed a desire at the early age of 15 to enter a convent for religious life; Vicka and her family were known for their very vocal and vigorous prayers. But generally, these youth were no different than most young people of the village or other teenagers of today.

As a result of the apparitions during the last 10 years, millions of young people have turned to the holy light of God instead of the darkness and despair of the world. In an age filled with the snares of drugs, alcohol, sex, broken families and materialism, these young converts are an evident sign of the good fruit of Medjugorje.

Michael O'Brien is one such young person who was uniquely led to this light of God. His story exemplifies the huge struggle for the young people of today. It is a struggle between Satan and God for the very future of the world.

Michael is a rock musician in Cleveland, Ohio, whose career and life took an unexpected turn in March, 1988. While watching a videotape of the apparitions of Medjugorje, he became convinced that it was authentic. He insisted that his parents go there to experience it first hand. What he didn't count on was his own acceptance to accompany them when asked by his mother if he wanted to go.

"I was the last one from my family anyone would have thought would go to Medjugorje," Michael stated. "In fact,

I was the last one of the kids my mom asked if I wanted to go. I was into the rock music business, you know—all of it; its good side and its bad side. Of all the kids in our family, I was the least religious, which is an understatement! But for some reason, I said yes."

In a whirlwind of mini-miracles in obtaining passports, visas and airline tickets, the O'Briens—including their "least religious" son Michael—found themselves a few weeks later on pilgrimage to the little hamlet where Our Lady was reportedly appearing.

The family spent the first few days like everyone else wandering around the village and climbing the hills. Michael went with them but didn't spend much time in church. It was only when they went to visit the visionary Vicka along with the rest of their pilgrim group, that his Medjugorje experience truly began.

"We were standing around after Vicka had spoken to our group and answered questions. She was busy signing autographs when all of a sudden, she stopped, asked for a pen from one of our group and began writing furiously on a small piece of paper," Michael recalled, shaking his head at the remembrance. "She then gave me the note and said it was a message from Our Lady for me. I was stunned and not really believing any of this. It was in Croatian, so I had no idea what it said. As soon as I could, I had it translated by our guide: *With your ability and talent, you can lead young people to God.*"

Michael experienced other mystical occurrences during the rest of his trip. But upon returning to his home in Cleveland, to the more familiar world of rock and roll music, the strange incident and the note itself were soon forgotten.

In September of that year, I was in Cleveland to give a series of talks on Medjugorje, having been invited by a strong advocate of the Medjugorje message, Jack Weiland.

Jack told me about Michael and about the incident with the note. I had heard so many stories connected with Medjugorje, that it was just that—another story.

"But you've got to meet this kid, Wayne," Jack said several times during the first days of my tour. "I really think Our Lady is going to use him to get to other young people. He's a good kid and he has been given a special task; he just doesn't know it yet!"

A few days later, Jack arranged for Michael to join us at a talk. He had asked Michael to come to the Mass that would precede the talk, and then to join us for dinner with the resident priest. This way, he felt, I could get to know him better and maybe get him involved.

About half-way through the opening of the Mass, Michael arrived, clumping down the side aisle to where we were seated. He slipped in the pew next to me and Jack whispered quick introductions. I looked at him and lightly shook my head; he was dressed in black, tight jeans with a black leather jacket to match, an earring in his ear and long, flowing black curly hair.

"This is the kid Jack thinks is going to turn others on to Medjugorje?" I thought to myself. I was totally unimpressed.

As we sang a hymn, I noticed that Michael was not singing. "I thought you were a singer," I said, nudging him.

"I don't sing hymns," he answered bluntly.

At the dinner with the priest, it was more of the same. I did not share Jack's enthusiasm about this young man. At Jack's urging, he related the story of the note for me and the priest. I asked him why he didn't follow up with what had been given to him if he thought it was from the Virgin Mary. He just shrugged his shoulders.

That evening during the talk, I really zeroed in on my new young acquaintance. I talked about the ill effects that rock music had on so many young people, looking directly at Michael who was perched on the floor in the standing-room- only packed church. He squirmed a little.

Afterwards, quite by accident as neither myself or Michael knew of the plans arranged by Jack, we ended up going to the O'Briens' home for refreshments. On arriving, there was Michael, as surprised to see me as I was him. But for some reason he kept hanging around me. In a short while we found ourselves sitting across from each other at the kitchen table.

"Mike," I suddenly blurted out, "Why didn't you do something about that note? I mean, if it's really from the Virgin Mary—don't you know there are some beautiful religious songs? For instance, *Gentle Woman;* that's a song Our Lady says she really likes."

Michael looked at me somewhat startled that I would ask such a question at this particular time. "I don't know; maybe I will someday." He got up and walked away.

I returned home and several weeks later, received an audio cassette tape in the mail. It was from Michael O'Brien. On it was the most beautiful singing of *Gentle Woman* I had ever heard. I sat there with chills—and tears as I realized that once again, Our Lady had used me to get to one of her beloved young people.

Soon, an entire casette of *five* religious songs, interspersed with actual sounds and recording of interviews with the visionaries arrived in the mail. It was called "Sounds of Medjugorje"; Michael's name was nowhere on the tape or jacket cover, but he was the one singing the songs.

I discovered later that this young man, moved by the few direct words I had spoken at his parents' home had single-handedly put this tape together, unbeknownst to the rest of his rock music group and manager. Thousands of copies would end up circulating around the world.

In the past two years, Michael O'Brien has sung his songs and witnessed to youth everywhere. He is fulfilling the beautiful message given him by Mary Virgin at Medjugorje. He still dresses and looks the same as on the first day we met. And the kids love him! He is bringing them to God with his ability and talent.

"Dear children, you know we are living The Year of the Young People. This year ends on August 15. Your Mother wishes to dedicate one more year to the youth. Not only to the youth, may this year also be the Year of the Family. Dear Children, in these days before the 15th of August, prepare yourselves, you and your family, for the new year to come so it may be the Year of the Family." —July 10, 1989

I have related how helpless and frustrated I was with my eldest son Steve. From my talks I know there are countless other parents equally distraught with their own wayward children. I've given the word of my testimony, of how God works in the hearts and lives of the children of devoted, praying parents. Now here is the testimony of one of those children who grieved—and then brought joy—to a mother's heart:

Dear Mr. Weible,
My mother received one of your newsletters from her (other) son at Fort Bragg, N. C., where he is stationed as a sergeant. This is testimony why (she received the newsletter).
In November of 1988, she went to Medjugorje with one of her sisters. My mother had trouble with walking, but she climbed up and down Cross

Mountain with no problem. I found out later that she went there to pray for her ten children.

That Christmas, I didn't even go to my parents' house for Christmas. I was too far-gone on cocaine, and drunk all the time. Two or three days after Christmas, my parents came to my apartment with some gifts. I told them I couldn't talk right now and they left the gifts and went home. I couldn't even look at them when walking them to the door. I looked up only to see a mother that was real worried about her son. I didn't know she was at Medjugorje the previous month, praying for all her children. I just kept remembering her worried look.

Of course, New Year's Eve arrived and I couldn't stay up. I never stopped (drugs and drinking) since Christmas. My body hurt; I couldn't think straight.

About four days after New Year's Eve, something hit me. I was alone and I asked God to help me. I asked Him to take this evil from me. I can't remember the exact words, but I pleaded for help from God.

The next thing I did was clean up the ashtrays, beer cans, everything from the previous party. From that moment of January, 1989, till now, I was cured of three heavy addictions: cocaine, alcohol and cigarettes—all in one prayer. I know my mother's prayer was answered from the mountain (in Medjugorje), because she loved her children so much.

In September of 1989, I moved in with my parents to get back on my feet again, with past debts to pay and etc. It was a blessing for my mother to see me around again, happy and straight. I fell in love with reading the Bible, now I wouldn't shut-up about all the teachings in the Bible. Everything I talked about was Jesus.

Well, at this time, we had received the newsletter from my brother. My mother loved it, so I read it and I loved it. So I saw the address on the back and ordered a subscription.

What I haven't told you yet in this letter, is that my mother had died July 29, 1990. She had cancer and was undergoing chemotherapy treatments during the year. Christmas that year was great for her. I lived at home with them, and I bought all my brothers and sisters a holy Bible. I saw a happiness in both parents that I (had) never seen before. In January of 1990, the doctor said the chemo might cease if she continues doing well. Well, by April, I moved out. My mother's condition worsened and by June, she was hospitalized and in July, she died.

For the eight months that I lived with her, we talked endlessly and I heard her mention my life as a complete miracle. When she died, I know she died with contentment. She's at peace now with no pain or crying. We all miss her very much.

> In Jesus name,
> Mark

New York

"Dear children, you know that I desire to lead you on the way of holiness, but I will not compel you to be saints by force. I desire that each of you by your own little self- denials help yourself and me so I can lead you from day to day to holiness. Therefore, dear children, I do not desire to force you to observe the messages. But rather this long time that I am with you is a sign that

I love you immeasurably, and what I desire of each individual is to become holy."—October 9, 1986

Dear Wayne,

Last night, I had the wonderful opportunity to hear you speak at St Patrick's Church in Edina. It was an extremely moving evening in many ways.

My name is Susan and I'm 26 years old. I'm the woman with shoulder-length blond hair that approached you at the end of the evening, and you gave me encouragement that I really needed to hear. It was like a pat on the back and someone saying to me that the work I am doing for the young people of this world really is important.

It is hard for me to convey to anyone just how much Medjugorje has impacted my life. The evening at St Patrick's was the closest I've come to actually being there.

I had read that you were coming to town the Sunday before, in the bulletin from church. About five minutes earlier, a dear friend of ours, Father Peter Christensen, who had just returned from Medjugorje, said he had something for us. We followed him into the sacristy where he presented us with two beautiful "peace rosaries" that had been blessed at St James Church in Medjugorje by Our Lady. His gift touched us both very deeply.

I was very excited at the possibility of hearing you speak (I never thought I'd get the chance). As I awoke Saturday morning, I was somewhat excited as I thought of all the things that were in store for me that day. I was late, though as I rushed out the door and when I returned, I had just about an hour to get to Edina for the book-signing. When I finally did meet you, my mind went blank, even though I had so much I wanted to tell you. I was just happy to meet you and thought maybe I'd get a chance to speak more to you that evening.

When we got to St Patrick's, I could hardly believe my eyes! The church was already packed! I could not find even a folding chair seat. I was thrilled that so many came, and finally found a tiny ledge to sit on near the floor. It was rather uncomfortable but I didn't care—I was just elated to be there.

The peace I felt when we all began to pray was incredible. Everything you said seemed to have direct meaning to the events in my life. You answered questions before I could ask them! It was simply amazing.

Mary knew that I needed your words of encouragement (in spreading this message among young people). Sometimes I'm overwhelmed with the scope of the problems that young people face today. I need to remember that I'm doing some good just by being there for them. I don't always know the right thing to say or do, but my love is the greatest gift I can give them. I'm renewed now, to go out and spread the message to everyone.

After I left you, I felt the intense desire to pray. I just did not want the evening to end. I found my way to the chapel, and I felt a strong need to pray the rosary. Being brought up Protestant and being a recent convert (a year ago) I learned that this is the most beautiful prayer of all. When I pray it from the heart, a peace comes over me that I can hardly describe.

Lately though, I have found myself forgetting that peace and making excuses not to pray it. Instead, I have been simply meditating free-form as I call it with no real direction.

Anyway, I decided to offer up my prayers and petitions for peace in the world. As I began to meditate on the joyful mysteries, a quiet peace began to envelop me. I prayed as I have never prayed before. When I got to the presentation of Jesus in the temple, I asked Our Lady to present me to the Lord—my soul, my body, my will, my life.

Suddenly, as I began to say the Glory Be, I saw a brief but radiant picture of Jesus. He was suspended above a rocky place; a brilliant light was behind Him and He was holding a book. At first, I thought it must be the Bible, but then I realized it was the Book of Life. At the same time, I had a feeling of being one with everything and everyone. I then passed out or something.

The next thing I remember is being slammed—and I mean slammed—back into consciousness. I found myself slumped over the pew in front of me; my rosary had dropped to the floor and my legs were sprawled out behind me. The immediate thought on my mind was the extreme urgency of the messages that the Blessed Virgin Mary has given us, at Medjugorje.

Shaking like a leaf, I picked the rosary off the floor without even thinking. My fingers were on the exact bead where I had left off, almost as if nothing had happened. I finished the last decade in a pure sense of joy at what had happened. I immediately knew that I had to share this with you.

May our Lord bless you with many special blessings and may Mary continue to give you guidance in all that you do.

Love and peace,
Susan

Minnesota

"Today I would like to invite you to constant prayer and penance. Particularly, have the young people of this parish become more active in their prayer."—July 26, 1983

I met a young man from Ireland in Medjugorje on one of my trips and while having a cold drink with him, we began talking about how young people seemed to be in such large numbers among the pilgrimages here. He was the coordinator for a Irish travel agency and had been living in the village for more than three months during the summer. Eventually, I got around to asking him how he had become involved in Medjugorje.

He looked at me and smiled somewhat sheepishly. "To tell you the truth, I came here to get a good tan, what with the weather we have in Ireland." I laughed and urged him to tell me more. "Well, my mom and dad had come here, and when they returned home, they wanted all of their children to come. I resisted, not really believing it all. But, you know to make them happy, and needing a good job, I took an offer to come here and coordinate the groups coming from Ireland. I didn't really know a lot about it, but figured it would be a good vacation, and besides, I'd get paid!"

How Our Lady uses the things of the world to attract young people to her message, I thought to myself as I listened.

"After a week or so here, something happened inside of me," the young Irishman continued, turning serious. "I truly felt what my parents had been talking about and for the first time in my life, Jesus was real. I realized also that I hadn't done a great deal of good in my life and now I had the chance. I can't thank the Blessed Mother enough for what is happening to young people here."

My young Irish friend not only assisted now with youth groups from Ireland but had given many talks throughout Ireland. His life was now totally dedicated to spreading the messages.

"Do not be in anxiety. May peace unite your hearts. Every disorder comes from Satan."—*August 15, 1983*

Dear Wayne Weible,

I don't expect you to receive this letter as I am sure you are very busy. I had the pleasure of reading your book and since first hearing about Medjugorje last year, I have felt drawn by the things I have read.

While reading your book, (I feel) the Holy Spirit let me know the truth and sincerity of your experience; God truly is working miracles every-day if we just look around us. Since hearing about Medjugorje, I have wanted to visit the place, but I don't have the finances.

It's strange, but within the week it took me to read your book, I felt spiritually close to you and the people you wrote about. You many not know me personally, but I have found yet another friend through the works done in Jesus' name.

I am 25 years old and am looking for peace
that others have found (through Medjugorje).
That may be all that young people are looking
for, but they are looking to drugs and other things
instead of God.

> Yours in Jesus,
> Claudia

Florida

*"I am with you even if you are not conscious of it. I want
to protect you from everything that Satan offers you and through
which he wants to destroy you. As I bore Jesus in my womb,
so also, dear children, do I wish to bear you unto holiness.
God wants to save you and sends you messages through men,
nature, and so many things which can only help you to
understand that you must change the direction of your life.
Therefore, little children, understand also the greatness of the
gift which God is giving you through me, so that I may protect
you with my mantle and lead you to the joy of life."—March
25, 1990*

Dear Wayne,

I feel that it is very important that all of us who
are involved in the ever-growing circle of the
blessings of Our Lady of Medjugorje to stay in
touch.

I think you will remember Misty, the 13-year-
old who began receiving music and lyrics after
having been to Medjugorje the summer of 1989. I
sent you one of her tapes and we met a couple of
times.

Missteps ministry has continued to grow rapidly

over the last two years. We sold 600 tapes in five months and gave away many to those who needed one. There are so many stories of blessings I could relate to you which have come our way through the giving of these tapes. She is doing concerts in and out of town.

The Catholic community has kept her busy. They are fascinated by the fact that we are Protestant and Baptist; and so in love with Mary!

Misty is 15 now, and very devoted to her calling to spread God's word and Mary's messages to as many as possible. She ministers in the high school were she attends. Our Blessed Mother and Lord have been leading us for two years now and what a wonderful trip it has been.

Wayne, this is a very unusual situation; Our Lady chose a 13-year-old girl to spread her word through music. This has been continuing to grow ever stronger for us.

Our Love,
Gwen (Misty's mother)

Texas

Finally, there is the story of the mother who took her troublesome 16-year-old daughter to Medjugorje, hoping it would help her. After three days of attending church, praying the rosary, and climbing the hills, the teenager implored her mother to leave the tour early and return to Ireland. In a word, she related to her mum, she was bored!

Four days later as our tour group headed back to Ireland, the young girl remained in Medjugorje; she had persuaded her mother to let her stay two additional weeks. It is as if Our Lady says to us, *"Send to Me your youth; I am a mother and I know how to love them and to convert them. . ."*

In the same way, you younger men [and women] must be obedient to the elders. In your relations with one another, clothe yourselves with humility, because God "is stern with the arrogant but to the humble he shows kindness." Bow humbly under God's mighty hand, so that in due time he may lift you high. Cast all your cares on him because he cares for you. Stay sober and alert. Your opponent the devil is prowling like a roaring lion looking for someone to devour. [I Peter 5:5-8]

9

Beloved Sons and Daughters

"The priests should visit families, more particularly those who do not practice anymore, and who have forgotten God. Priests should carry the Gospel of Jesus to the people, and teach them how to pray. And the priests themselves should pray more and also fast. They should give to the poor what they don't need."—May 30, 1984

The man approached me at the end of a luncheon that had been arranged for me to meet with a gathering of priests from around the city. It had been a busy event-filled tour, occupying my time day and evening.

I didn't know who this stranger was; he wasn't wearing a priest's collar, and I was sure he wasn't with the group that had sponsored my trip.

"Excuse me, Mr. Weible," he began somewhat hesitant, "I wondered if I could speak with you for a minute?" I was anxious to return to the hotel for some quiet time before the talk that evening. There hadn't been much in the last few days. But seeing his anxiety I replied that I would be glad to give him a few minutes.

In the next half-hour, in a quiet corner of the room I learned that the stranger was a priest who had left the

Church. In painful forced tones, he related to me how he had deserted his priesthood to live with a woman whom he felt he was in love with. He fully intended to marry her; but it never happened. As is so often the case with such occurrences, the woman who was the reason for this priest renouncing his vows was an active member of his parish.

The ever-present guilt and adjustments to life outside the Church had kept him in turmoil. And then he learned of the apparitions of Our Lady at Medjugorje. It triggered within him a full realization of the gift of priesthood that God had given him; he immediately felt an urgency to repent and renew his vows. The affair with the woman came to an abrupt halt.

In a quiet voice he asked me to pray for him and for his request for reinstatement to the Church to be approved. "All I can say is that I have been deeply touched by what is happening at Medjugorje and now I want to return to my priesthood. Please—pray for me and my intentions!" With that, he thanked me for the time and left the room.

How often we think of Medjugorje's miracle of conversion to God as being for the lay person; why would a priest need conversion? Is he not a representative of Jesus Himself? The same can be said for the thousands of women throughout the world who give their lives to Jesus and to service for others. It is a hard, demanding life of commitment, and many, unable to live up to its spiritual standards, end up leaving the order. For some reason, many of us assume that once they've taken their vows, they're saved and well on their way to heaven.

Dozens of personal conversations and experiences with priests and nuns, not to mention scores of letters, have proven to me that these beloved sons and daughters of the Church need conversion just as much as we do; actually, because of their commitment, they need it at even greater depth. In these discussions and letters, almost everyone of them confesses that at some point in their lives as priests or nuns, they have seriously considered giving it up for a "normal" life.

One such story stands out above the others—that of Father Jim Waters, of Wilmington, North Carolina.

I met Father Jim through Karen Stoffel, who lived in Wilmington, had journeyed to Medjugorje, and returned with a special and determined mission: she wanted to get all the priests in her area interested or involved in the apparitions of Medjugorje. The daughter of Jim and Rosie Stoffel who had been so instrumental in my introduction to Medjugorje, Karen now called to ask a favor: Would I be willing to come to Wilmington, which was only 80 miles away, to speak with the five priests assigned there, say, at a dinner at her home? I replied that I would.

After several scheduled and then cancelled dates, due to the "busy" schedule of one or more of the priests, she called me again. "How about a luncheon, instead of a dinner?" she asked with enthusiasm. "They have to eat sometime, and this is my last hope!"

Again, I told her just to let me know when.

Several weeks later I was sitting in Karen's home, listening to her describe the different priests and which ones she thought might go to Medjugorje. I had informed her that I was taking a tour over in a couple of months and still did not have a spiritual leader. I had asked my own Lutheran pastor, and he declined—as did the Catholic priest and all others I had asked.

"Well, there's only one I'm absolutely sure won't go," she said. "That's Father Jim Waters—he's in to some strange things and doesn't believe any of this Medjugorje stuff. The only reason he is coming to the lunch is because I help him out at his church periodically."

Soon there was a knock at the door. Karen asked me

to get it since she was busy in the kitchen. I opened the door and saw a huge man, standing 6'4" or so, and weighing close to 250 pounds.

"How ya doin?" he exclaimed. "You must be the guy involved in this apparition thing. Gotta tell ya, I don't believe it!"

In the next half hour I was sure that this fast-talking, New York City native who dominated the conversation, had to be the most obnoxious priest I had ever met!

We had a nice lunch; then I spoke to them about Medjugorje and what it had done to my life. After a few questions and a noticeable hesitancy on the part of the majority of them, I said, "I have a tour going to Medjugorje in a couple of months and I really need some spiritual leadership; I'd like to invite one—or all of you—to go as my special guest. The trip is free. All you have to do is get a passport and the time off."

One by one they politely thanked me and gave reasons why they could not go—all except one: Father Jim Waters, the last one I thought would accept.

"Hey, that's great!" he declared. "You know, I think I'll go with you. It should be interesting!"

I drove home in a daze. This was not what I had expected. In fact, I had even prayed that he would not accept, almost sure of his answer because of what Karen had said about him. But here I was, stuck with this odd priest as my spiritual leader.

Two months later, we arrived in Chicago for our flight to Dubrovnik, where we would then take a bus to the little village. Father Jim grabbed me as soon as I arrived at the airport, giving me a long lists of things he wanted: leg room on the plane, a private room in Medjugorje, et cetera. Well, at least he was wearing his collar!

Suddenly a woman from the tour group came up and grabbed Father Jim by the sleeve. "Father, I got to talk to you—now!" Try as he might, Father Jim could not persuade her to wait until they arrived in Medjugorje; she wanted him to hear her confession before boarding the airplane. Two hours later, he returned, pale and shaken. "That's the most difficult—and beautiful—confession I have ever heard!"

I didn't hear much from the good father for the next three days. We had arrived and settled in; I only saw Father Jim at the altar for the English-speaking Mass. On the third morning I was shocked to see him rise to read the gospel. Fully expecting that machine-gun staccato style, I sat there stunned, as he read it slowly and reverently.

Later that afternoon as we were returning from a group visit to Vicka's home where we heard her speak and answer questions, Father Jim caught up with me on the pathway through the fields. "Listen," he started, "I just wanted to thank you for inviting me here. I don't really believe that these kids are seeing Mary, but I do believe that the Holy Spirit is present; this is a holy place!"

Four days later, as we headed home, Father Jim Waters had been completely converted to the authenticity of Medjugorje. He now did believe that the young visionaries were experiencing apparitions. And much of his conversion had come from hearing hours of confessions from the depths of hearts touched and convicted as never before. Every day for the remaining days since our little conversation, he had been hearing confessions. He returned to his parish a different priest. And his parishioners could not believe the transformation!

Several weeks went by and one afternoon I received a telephone call from my wonderfully-changed priest. "Wayne, you've got to come to my parish and speak about Medjugorje—how about this weekend?"

"Okay, okay," I laughed. If this priest made good on half of what he had promised concerning Medjugorje. . .

Filled with the spirit of the little village, he had announced as we arrived home that one day he would return to Medjugorje with a chartered plane filled with at least 300 North Carolinians, the bishop, a news team, and more.

That Saturday evening after the Mass and my talk at his church, we were driving to the rectory for dinner. Father Jim had become unusually silent. "How come you're so quiet?" I asked. "It's not like you!"

"Wayne, I have to tell you something," he began in a low voice. "Before I went with you to Medjugorje. . . I had no faith. I've been a priest for 22 years. Do you have any idea what it's like to stand at that altar day after day, holding up those gifts of the Blessed Sacrament—and not believe?"

"Father, you mean your faith had diminished, don't you?" I stammered, embarrassed by this confession.

He pulled the car over to the side of the road and slammed his hand hard on the dashboard. "No! I mean *I had no faith! No faith!*"

Less than a year later, Father Jim Waters was in a head-on automobile accident that crushed every bone in his chest and caused severe head injuries. He lay in a coma in the hospital, expected to die at any moment. He did not die. It took two and a half years of rehabilitation and struggle, but he beat the odds and is now assigned as an assistant priest with limited duties, in a small town in North Carolina.

Father Jim did not take three hundred people to Medjugorje; but he did charter a plane and take close to 200, including members of the Bishop's office and a full television crew. Before his accident, he gave talks all over North Carolina. Now, although he does not remember going to Medjugorje, his faith, his priesthood, and his commitment to service to others, are still there and still strong.

There are many other Father Jim Waters throughout the world who need the spiritual renewal that Medjugorje offers to the beloved sons and daughters. And as long as Our Lady remains, they too, will be among the converted.

"Pray more for your spiritual life. Do your utmost in this sense. Pray for your Bishop."—August 12, 1983

Dear Mr. Weible,

I have just finished reading your book, I've had two copies for almost a year. Two of my parishioners gave them to me but after numerous attempts to read it, they ended up at the bottom of a stack of others to be read later.

The problem, you see, is that I was never really interested in Medjugorje. My curiosity was sparked when people would return with rosaries that had turned to a golden color, and tales of visions in the sun, but other than that, I had better things to occupy my thoughts.

For the past several years, I've been working with a travel agent in leading pilgrimages to the Holy Land and various Marian shrines in Europe. For some time now she has been asking me to take a group to Medjugorje. Finally, a year ago, more out of a sense of friendship than anything else, I decided to say yes.

As the date of departure drew closer, more and more I regretted my decision to go. I tried to convince myself that I was going with an open mind but by the time we flew into Dubrovnik, my skepticism was complete.

I must confess that the first few days in

Medjugorje didn't help change my mind. The crowds, the shops, the various national groups lining up to say Mass reminded me of airplanes ready for takeoff—I just knew it was a big mistake coming here. I should not have been expecting anything, and yet I felt disappointed. The past year had been a particularly difficult one for me.

First of all, my prayer life was in ruins. As hard as I tried, I just couldn't seem to be consistent in praying the Liturgy of the Hours. And of course, everything else seemed to crumble along with it. The only thing that kept me going was the Eucharist, and I was beginning to lose my grip even on that. So you see, although I wasn't a firm believer in Medjugorje, I suppose deep down I was hoping that there might be something to it. I needed something to happen—and soon.

It did happen. On Friday morning—which just happened to be the first Friday of the month—we decided to make the Way of the Cross up Mount Krizevac. We began the climb at 6:00 a.m. to avoid the heat of the day. The ascent was long and slow, as a number of our group were impeded by age and/or weakness. At first, I felt very impatient wondering why didn't those who were having such difficulty just stay at home if they were having such trouble.

By the fifth station of the cross, my patience was wearing thin. As I turned to see where our laggards were, I saw two men carrying an elderly lady step by step over the sharp stones. I turned to begin the reflection on the station, thinking if I wait for her, we'll be here all day. I lifted my eyes to the station and saw Simon carrying our Lord's cross, and people surrounding Jesus, yelling at

Him to hurry up. Quickly, I turned again to look at the lady taking one painful step at a time, and my heart almost broke. I waited for them to reach us and continued the meditation as my eyes began to fill with tears.

At the next station I offered her my bottle of water and asked if she might not want to sit and wait for us at this station, reassuring her that we would pick her up on our way down. Her legs were sore, her face flushed and by now the sun was beating down on us. "Just one more station, Father," she pleaded, panting, "just one more station."

After each successive station, I would look back at her and her lips would move, "Just one more station, Father."

That became for me one of the most powerful sermons I had ever heard. When we finally reached the top of the mountain, I struggled up the last few yards to the foot of the cross, folded my arms on its base and laid my head on my arms to say an Our Father for all of the people from my parish who had asked me to pray for them. Oddly enough, the only thing that came to my mind was my fellow priests in my diocese, then my own priesthood and a shocking sense of my sins and infidelities to that priesthood.

Tears began to run down my cheeks. This is where the priesthood belongs, I thought; this is where I've been running from—the foot of the Cross.

I had once asked God to make me a good priest. I hadn't thought of asking Him to make me a holy priest. Perhaps I was afraid of what it would cost. I began to sob; they were deep, long, painful sighs of remorse. It was like a pressure bearing down on me. Like a winepress pressing out every bit of the juice from the grapes.

After a little while, I left my spot and walked to a little secluded spot where I could be alone and pray. I really prayed from my heart. It was something I had not done in years.

Our little group began making its way back down the mountain, each person at their own pace. This time, the Lord gave me the honor of being a Simon of Cyrene to another elderly lady. It cost, as my back ached and my arms throbbed as I had to help her with almost each step. But somewhere along the way, I became aware of an all-embracing overwhelming sense of peace—a "peace that the world cannot give."

Since returning home, the graces continue. The first thing I did was to get rid of my television and VCR (a strong addiction). My prayer life is now full and alive. I go to bed each night so tired that I feel as though I've been beaten. And yet, I am so thankful to our Blessed Mother and her Son, Jesus, for yet another beautiful day.

I do not believe it was by accident that I did not read your book before going to Medjugorje. Now that I've read it, I have confirmation of the things I have seen and felt for myself.

May God continue to bless you and your family.

Father Ken

Canada

"The Mass is the greatest prayer of God. You will never be able to understand its greatness. That is why you must be perfect and humble at Mass, and you should prepare yourselves there."—December, 1983

Dear Mr. Weible,

Several months ago, I was privileged to attend one of your presentations on Medjugorje. You spoke at All Saints Catholic Church in Detroit.

I especially remember two things about which you spoke. First, that Medjugorje was not meant to be merely a geographical phenomenon. Medjugorje is to happen all over the world. (You said) The same resurgence of prayer, fasting, and conversion is to happen throughout the world.

Another part of your witness that I especially remember from that evening is how you spoke about the Eucharist. You said that you ache to receive the Eucharist, but are unable because of being a Lutheran. Your testimony only helps me to appreciate Eucharist more, not to dismiss it as merely Catholic ritual action. I have been a Catholic all my life, and a Franciscan for the past eleven years. I am now a deacon, and look forward to being ordained a priest in June.

After I listened to your presentation I purchased the "Rosary on Cassette" and (now) try to pray it daily. Before, I was unable to consistently pray it. When war broke out in the Gulf, we began Monday night prayer services in our parish for peace. We prayed the rosary as a congregation. Wayne, It was incredible how after attending your presentation in Detroit, how many people talked with me about the rosary. I neither initiated the conversations or told them we were praying it in our parish, nor about my own change of heart toward this style of prayer. The subject of the rosary kept coming up. I took those "coincidences" as a movement of the Spirit calling us to pray and seek the intercession of Mary.

I want you to know I am grateful to you and for you. I have but one favor to ask you: when you go to Medjugorje again, could you please pray for my vocation to the priesthood? This would mean a great deal to me. Somehow, I feel Mary will be integral in my priestly ministry.

Peace...

Bob

Michigan

The following message was given in answer to a specific request for information by a Medjugorje priest:

"The information suffices. People already know enough. Tell them this place is a place of prayer. Pray as much as you can, pray however you can, but pray more always. Each of you could pray even four hours a day. But I know that many do not understand because they think only of living for their work."—April 24, 1984

Dear Wayne,

How ashamed of myself I am! I wrote you a week or so ago and asked if I could go to Medjugorje when you go, that is, on one of your tours that you go with on occasion. How selfish on my part for I have already been once.

Also, a travel agency asked me to be a spiritual leader for a group of pilgrims going to Medjugorje. I asked my Provincial team and got their permission and blessing. But guess I got impatient since the agency was holding off because of the war in the Gulf, and now the internal struggle going on in Yugoslavia.

May I ask you instead that if you have any speaking engagements in Detroit, and your schedule allows, that you stop by our retirement center for our sisters of Mercy to speak to them? I have shown your video and some others are ordering it. I am also reading your book to a blind sister.

I trust that you and your family will experience the joy and peace of Easter. Thank you again for responding to Mary's call and allowing God to work through you.

Prayerfully,
Sister Annita

Michigan

"Thank you for all your sacrifices!"—June 25, 1984

Father Don had Multiple Sclerosis—so badly that there was a real question, as to whether the trip to Medjugorje would be too much for him. The terrain was rugged, the conditions primitive. There was no way he could ever make it up Podbrdo, let alone Mt. Krizevac! But I was taking four other priests and two other Lutheran ministers, including my minister of music, and he wanted to go so badly. . . In the end I prayed about it and sensed that the Blessed Mother wanted him to come, in spite of his affliction (or perhaps because of it).

He came. and he even went up Mt. Krizevac, carried

by his four brothers in the priesthood. This is the letter he wrote:

Dear Wayne,

Thank your very much for being a willing instrument of the Lord in my having gone to Medjugorje in October, 1990. Praise God!

The memories of my having been there have grown stronger, rather than weaker in the almost two months that have passed since then. Medjugorje was a high point of my life. I realize it all the more now. Not only has Our Lady helped me to have an ever-improving feeling and attitude about my Multiple Sclerosis, but she has injected a deeper vitality into my prayer life as well. Praise God.

Thank you for the wonderful opportunity to meet so many of the Lord's fine people. You are an instrument of the Lord.

God's peace always,
Father Don

New Mexico

"When I say pray, pray, pray, I do not want to say only to increase the number of hours of prayer, but also to reinforce the desire for prayer, and to be in contact with God. Place yourself permanently in a state of spirit bathed in prayer."—June 26, 1984

Dear Wayne,

I wish words could express thoughts and feelings adequately; I am so grateful for having gone to Medjugorje. I will never be the same. It was the greatest week of my life.

My religious superiors are very reluctant to allow international travel, and they weren't real excited about me going to Medjugorje, but they did say yes, for which I am grateful. Even though I may never get back there, I will cherish those days for the rest of my life.

Being there with you was such an added blessing. Our Little Huntington group will continue to pray together and share our thoughts as time goes on. Everyone cherished their days there.

May God bless you, your wife and your family. My prayers and love come your way each day, especially at Mass and rosary time.

Christ's love,
Father Ron

Indiana

"I pray for the priests and the parishioners, that no one may be troubled. I know the changes which will take place soon [in the parish clergy at Medjugorje]. At the time of the changes, I will be there. Also, do not be afraid; there will be in the future signs concerning sinners, unbelievers, alcoholics, and young people. They will accept me again."

When they had eaten their meal, Jesus said to Simon Peter, "Simon, son of John, do you love me more then these?" "Yes, Lord," he said, "You know that I love you." At which Jesus said, "Feed my lambs." [John 21:15]

10

A Message for all Faiths

"Those who are not Catholics, are no less creatures made in the image of God and destined to rejoin someday the House of the Father. Salvation is available to everyone, without exception. Only those who refuse God deliberately are condemned. To him who has been given little, little will be asked for. To whomever has been given much, very much will be required. It is God alone, in His infinite justice, who determines the degree of responsibility and pronounces judgment."— January, 1985

In the early weeks of the apparitions, the inevitable question was put to the young visionaries to ask the Blessed Virgin Mary: why are there so many faiths? Mirjana, who lived in Sarajevo and visited her grandmother in Medjugorje in the summers, was the one chosen to present the question. She seemed the likely choice since she lived in a city divided by three major faiths and the religion of Communism—atheism.

The extraordinary answer, so uniquely phrased, was as follows: *"My dear little ones, my Son and I do not cut the cake into pieces where faith is involved; we do not put the walls up that divide you; you have done that to yourselves. Rather,* we look into your hearts, for that is where true love of God and others is found."

After hesitating a moment, she gave Mirjana a motherly look of love and continued: *"Mirjana, I wish to lead you and the others to holiness; your neighbor, Pasha, is a good example of the holiness I desire of each of you."*

Mirjana, startled, exclaimed, "Blessed Mother, Pasha is a *Moslem!"*

Pausing and then smiling, Mary answered, *"Yes, I know; but that is for God to decide. You must work to take care of your own soul!"*

Can one imagine what would happen if we each worked to take care of our own soul? If we stopped judging one another? If we were suddenly able to accept, tolerate and truly love each other?

Our Lady was not saying that the Moslem faith was the true faith; She simply pointed out Pasha's *sincerity and devotion* to God as a true example of holiness. She indicated that we are to love, respect and tolerate one another. How can we evangelize our neighbor if we do not love him or respect his faith?

In later messages, Mary Virgin would have much to say concerning the quantity and diversity of so many faiths. She would indicate that it is no accident that she comes to us through children of the Catholic faith. And why not? From the early Church the Catholics have maintained a strong devotion and love for the mother of Jesus, fully corroborating the Scriptural text, "all ages to come shall call me blessed." [Luke 1:48]

In fact, a dominant theme in the messages from Mary is that she comes for *all* of the children of God. Her repeated calls for prayer, fasting and penance is meant to heal our divisions and to make us fully understand the Scriptural reference in Ephesians that reads: "There is but one body and one Spirit, just as there is but one hope given all of you by your call. There is one Lord, one faith, one baptism, and one God and Father of all, who is over all, and works through all, and is in all." [Eph. 4:4-6]

Despite a predominantly Catholic following throughout the ten years of daily apparitions at Medjugorje, there are now significant numbers of non-Catholics included in the many pilgrimages to the little village. Protestants are accepting the apparitions as a true sign of God's love; Christian book stores which normally never carry more than a minimal amount of "Catholic" material, are well-stocked with books on Medjugorje.

In this age of indulgence and secularism, the people of the world are spiritually starved. They hungrily seek out and hope that miracles like the apparitions at Medjugorje are from God. It was due to this hunger that I was able to take two Protestant clergy to Medjugorje in 1987; one was a Baptist minister. The other was a pastor of my own Lutheran faith.

At the end of our pilgrimage, there was hope from one, and despair from the other. The Baptist minister was filled with the spiritual exhilaration of what was happening to people at Medjugorje. He didn't change his theological beliefs—or his denomination—but he truly believed that God was actively involved in what was occurring there. My Lutheran pastor was upset from the first day. From his pre- pilgrimage reading he had imagined that this was a huge break-through in ecumenism. To his regret, he found that nothing had changed theologically. He spent the first three days of the pilgrimage locked in his room.

On the day before our departure for home, my Lutheran pastor was wandering aimlessly around the old city area of Dubrovnik, when our paths crossed unexpectedly. I was quietly savoring the last bits of the trip.

"You know, Wayne," he began as we settled in a small

street cafe for a cold drink, "I came here hoping to find real unity. I think that what I have found is that you must be Catholic to understand and accept the apparitions."

We talked for a long time as I tried to point out to him that each of us must evaluate what the phenomenon means to us and what we are to do with it in our lives. It was a long, and I thought at the time, fruitless conversation.

Several weeks later, I received letters from both of my fellow Protestants who had been exposed to this new chapter in their spiritual lives. The Baptist was back to being a Baptist; Medjugorje, which he explained in terms of Baptist theology, was merely an interesting exercise along the spiritual pathway.

Meanwhile, my Lutheran pastor had done a total about-face! Once he had reached home and had quiet time to think about all that he had witnessed, the entire experience had unfolded. Now he was boldly speaking out on Medjugorje to his congregation; he was even teaching Catholics, as well as non-Catholics, how to pray— including the rosary! He was, in essence, blossoming into the full bloom of joy and peace that comes from submission to God, even if that submission is not quite in line with previous theological opinion.

An important key to understanding and accepting such beautiful miracles of God as the apparitions at Medjugorje in this modern age lies in understanding the Messenger, Mary. My Lutheran pastor was able to do that. And he discovered, as I had, that Martin Luther, founder of our denomination—and Protestantism—*never lost his own devotion to Mary, the mother of Jesus!*

It is man's divisions, created by picking and choosing what is desired in belief, that cause us to lose such precious gifts. We continue to split apart like colonies of amoebae; we continue to allow Satan the satisfaction of using the very faith in Christ we all claim to have, to confuse and divide.

I cling to the hope that with the fruition of the Medjugorje messages, we will once again live like men in ancient times.

"Tell the faithful that I need their prayers, and prayers from all the people. It is necessary to pray as much as possible and do penance because very few people have been converted up until now. There are many Christians who live like pagans. There are always so few true believers." —1984

Dear Wayne,

I began reading your book two days ago and it is 4 A.M., and I have just finished it. I have to thank you and all of those around you for this book.

It was given to me by my very best friend, who is a Catholic (I'm not). She told me to just read it with an open mind. I am a very firm believer in God and Jesus, but until now, I knew nothing of the Blessed Virgin Mary. I've just finished asking for forgiveness, because I have never acknowledged her.

Your story has opened up a door for me that I didn't know existed. My desire to learn more is so overwhelming. I am praying for guidance.

I have been considering joining the Army as a Russian linguist. Tonight, I asked God to please guide me and direct me in the way of His will for me, as I am unsure as to what He thinks of this idea.

My mind was totally blown, twice. First, just before I took the language test, I asked Jesus for

guidance and told Him that if He thought it was
right for me, then please help me pass (the test). I
did—with flying colors. Secondly, I have been
thinking that learning Russian could help me
help the world find peace. Then, I read in your
book that one of the secrets at Fatima was that
Russia would be converted to Christianity!

So, I will just keep praying. I had never even
heard of this (Medjugorje) or any other
apparitions. My loves goes out to you. Thank you
and God bless you.

Your friend,
Polly

Connecticut

In December, 1984, the visionaries were given a question
to ask the Blessed Mother: "what about such forms of
Eastern meditation as Zen and Transcendental Meditation?" She replied:

*"Why do you call them 'meditations' when it deals with human
works? The true meditation is a meeting with Jesus. When you
discover joy, interior peace, you must know there is only one
God, and only one Mediator, Jesus Christ."*

It was late at night, and Terri had gone to bed when
the telephone rang. Rushing to pick it up, so as not to
wake Terri, I answered with obvious irritation at the
lateness of the call. "Hello, who is this?"

"Is this Wayne Weible, the Protestant who wrote this
book on Medjugorje?"

"Yes, what do you want?"

"Well, uh, listen, I'm sorry for calling so late—I forgot
what time it is in your area. I'm calling from Wyoming,

and I just finished reading your book, and I don't quite know what to do about it."

The ambiguity of the conversation added to my impatience. "Look: how can I help you?"

"Well, it's just that I believe this appearance of the Blessed Virgin Mary is really happening in Medjugorje, and—well, I'm an Assemblies of God minister—we're not supposed to believe in such things!"

My mood changed immediately, and we talked for the next 45 minutes; once again, the message of love and individual peace had captured the heart of a "good and faithful" servant.

Dear Mr. Weible,

After reading and re-reading your book, I feel compelled to write to you. It may seem strange for someone who has been a Lutheran all her life to have a devotion to Mary, but I was introduced to her when I was ten years old.

Moving into a predominantly Protestant area in Germany, I lost touch for several years. Attending prayer meetings at a Catholic church in Toronto, I was reintroduced to Marian devotion. Although I am still struggling with my relationship with Mary, I am totally convinced (and have always been) of the authenticity of her apparitions in Lourdes, Fatima and Medjugorje.

I feel that Mary is calling me into a deeper prayer life with her, but also to give more witness about her. This, as you can imagine, in my position as a Lutheran pastor is not easy; I could very quickly be called on the carpet for "heresy."

Mary's message is getting more urgent all the

time, as if time is running out. This is indicated in a number of books I have read recently.

I feel that those of us who believe in Mary's message for repentance, prayer, peace, etc., in order to bring people back into a true faith in her Son, Jesus Christ, stand in need of mutual support and understanding.

> With prayers and blessings,
> in Christ,
> Rev. Giselda Nolte

Quebec, Canada

In Medjugorje, in January of 1985, a Catholic priest was thrown into confusion by the miraculous healing of an Orthodox child. He asked the visionaries about this, and they asked the Blessed Mother. Her reply: *"Tell this priest, tell everyone, that it is you who are divided on earth. The Muslims and the Orthodox, for the same reason as Catholics, are equal before my Son and me. You are all my children. Certainly, all religions are not equal, but all men are equal before God, as St Paul says. It does not suffice to belong to the Catholic Church to be saved, but it is necessary to respect the commandments of God in following one's conscience."*

A woman pushed her way through the crowd at the front of the church where I was speaking, excitedly clutching a rosary in her hand. Interrupting a lady who was telling me of her trip to Medjugorje, she said, "Listen, I'm sorry for interrupting but the strangest thing happened to me while I was listening to you," she began excitedly with the start of tears beginning in each eye, mixing with the smile of wonderment on her face.

"Whoa, slow down!" I laughed, "what happened?"

"I was listening to you talk about the rosary when all

at once I felt like I was being asked to go to the back of the church and get a rosary. So I did. And I wanted to pay for it but this lady told me to just take it, and—" She paused long enough to catch her breath. "I just feel I'm being asked to pray it, but I don't know why and I don't know how to pray a rosary!"

"Well, that shouldn't be a problem," I answered. "I'm sure you prayed one when you were little and if you get a little booklet or ask someone in your family or the priest, it should come right back to mind."

"You don't understand!" She said, laughing and crying at the same time. "I'm a Southern Baptist—I've never prayed a rosary in my life!"

"Dear children, I wish you to be active in living and transmitting the messages."—June 5, 1986

Dear Wayne,

I was so happy upon finding your book about the messages from Mary in Medjugorje. It was especially appropriate for me, as I, too, am a non-Catholic. It was nice to hear a Protestant perspective, though I say that without any bias or prejudice toward any religion. Heretofore, any books or information that I found concerning Medjugorje have all been from the Catholic viewpoint.

I went to Medjugorje twice in June/August of 1988. On the June trip our group was accompanied by the 20/20 news team, and Martin Sheen. They have since made a documentary entitled "Medjugorje—The Lasting Sign."

After returning from the August trip, I did some serious rethinking and pretty much continued to live my life the same, but with the messages of Mary always in the back of my mind. I say that because it was difficult to share anything about my experiences verbally with family and friends (other than those that were Catholic), as they didn't understand what I was doing or why I was even involved in such activities having to do with the Catholic church. Today, on looking back, I'm not sure I knew either! So, I just tried to live the messages Mary gave us.

I've been reawakened and renewed and will now move forward. I now know that I wasn't crazy or strange to go there twice in one summer, that I was definitely led to Mary for a purpose. I know now that I can and will do what God has planned for me, whatever it may be.

God bless you!

Judy

Colorado

"Today, I invite you to decide for God and once again to choose Him before everything and above everything, so that He may work miracles in your life; and, that day by day, your life may become joy with Him. Therefore, little children, pray and do not permit Satan to work in your life through misunderstandings, not understanding, and not accepting one another. Pray that you may be able to comprehend the greatness and the beauty of the gift of life."—January 25, 1989

Hello Wayne,

I first heard of the apparitions of Mary at Medjugorje at our family picnic a few summers ago, from my sister who was visiting from her home in Italy. My heart trembled and rejoiced at the news. I wondered what it was all about. But I did not ask. When my husband and I became Lutheran 10 years ago, I no longer felt free to be Catholic and so my lifelong devotion to Mary went underground.

Since my arrival at the University of Regina in September (1990), for a sabbatical year of study, I read your book and wish to thank you most sincerely for having written it. I needed to know that Mary is for everybody and that I can come out of the closet. I understood last fall that my main task here is to live an intense spiritual renewal and to put my life in order. The practicum in counseling course is the tool and stage where this last is being done.

An old friend, a Jesuit, has been instrumental, first passing on your book and then informing me of Padre (Stefano) Gobbi's impending visit. I felt called to go to the airport to meet him and attended the Mass the following day, where I renewed my gift of self to Mary in the format Padre Gobbi presented.

I was deeply moved throughout and shortly became extremely fearful and began to tremble at the realization that I might have committed a sacrilege by pledging support of the Pope and the Magisterium. "I am a Lutheran now, that's where my life has led me and I think that's where Jesus wants me to be." And I waited for an answer.

An unexpected answer came: from my left a

pervading aroma of roses wound about me. Unmistakable. And I thought of the Little Flower (St Theresa of the Child Jesus). I realized a few days later that this was her feast day; she's my favorite saint. The smell dissipated after what seemed to be a few minutes. And then, wonder of wonders! The aroma of Mary's favorite flowers came in turn from my right: lily, rose, cyclamen. They then blended into one aroma and enveloped me.

Everyone about me seemed unknowing and unaffected. Upon checking within, I dismissed the possibility that I had engineered this mind-trick. Afterwards, I went around the whole church: not one of those flowers was there that night. I had to know.

And I walk with and rest in Mary since, listening and meditating on her words in "To Her Priests." She continues to lead me to Jesus, such that my whole being says: Jesus is mine.

I am not yet ready, not yet wholly what and who She needs me to be. So, I ask for humility, patience, and wisdom. I am thankful that She did not forget me at this late hour.

Please pray that my husband, a Lutheran pastor, be restored to health in the Lord's good time. The doctors think he has MS.

May the Father, the Son and the Holy Spirit keep you and yours.

> In Jesus and Mary,
> Elise

Canada

"Dear children, you are not aware of the messages which God is sending to you through me. He is giving you great graces and you are not grasping them. Pray to the Holy Spirit for enlightenment. If you only knew the greatness of the graces God was giving you, you would pray without ceasing."—November 8, 1984

Dear Wayne,

Although we have never met, I feel as though I know you as a brother in Christ. I am a born-again, Spirit-filled Christian travel agent, who knew little or nothing of the events in Medjugorje. A client came to me by referral with a testimony of miraculous healing while praying a rosary brought to her from Medjugorje. She wanted to make the pilgrimage, and thus began my search for details and knowledge.

The first book I read was yours. I was touched in my spirit and although I am not of the Catholic faith, I felt deep in my heart I was to lead a group. We have reserved 32 seats preparing to leave Portland in June, 1991.

Please pray with us for the will of the Lord concerning this trip. Although thousands of people make the trip, I somehow feel this particular group will be special. There will be a mix of devout Catholics, those who have not attended church in years, several Pentecostal believers, and those who simply are searching for peace and hope.

Knowing your terribly busy schedule, I felt almost guilty writing to you, but at the urging of

the Holy Spirit, I am following that still small
voice. Thank you for spreading the love of Jesus.

Cordially,

Pat

Oregon

*"You are responsible for the messages. The source of grace is
here, but you, dear children, are the vehicles transmitting the
gifts. Therefore, dear children, I am calling you to work
responsibly. Everyone will be responsible according to his own
measure. Dear children, I am calling you to give the gift to
others with love and not to keep it for yourselves."—May 8,
1986*

As I finished speaking one evening on my tour to
Singapore, a man clutching a rosary walked up to me;
he was escorted on each side by a security guard, causing
me to wonder what this was all about. All three of the
men looked very grave; had I done something wrong?

"Sir, you have touched my heart tonight," the man with
the rosary began, "And I want you to know that you have
also touched the hearts of these two young men who are
my sons; one is a Muslim and the other, a Hindu."

When a Samaritan woman came to draw water, Jesus said
to her, "Give me a drink." (His disciples had gone off
to town to buy provisions.) The Samaritan woman said
to him, "You are a Jew. How can you ask me, a Samaritan
and a woman, for a drink?" [Recall that Jews have nothing
to do with Samaritans.] Jesus replied: "If only you
recognized God's gift and who it is that is asking you for
a drink, you would have asked him instead, and he would
have given you living water." [John 4:7-10]

11

Not All Believe

"I give you advice: I would like you to try to conquer some fault each day. If your fault is to get angry at everything, try each day to get angry less. If your fault is not to be able to study, try to study. If your fault is not to be able to obey, or if you cannot stand those who do not please you, try on a given day to speak with them. If your fault is not to be able to stand an arrogant person, you should try to approach that person. If you desire that person to be humble, be humble yourselves. Show that humility is worth more than pride."—February 20, 1985

After reading this pointed message from Mary, I was tentative about including the letters and answers of this chapter in the book. Unlike the majority of letters and stories it contains, these are negative; they are a sampling from those who fail to see the good fruit from God that is being poured out on us from Medjugorje. Yet they are also a part of those I receive—a very small percentage of the total.

Therefore, I feel they should be included; not to defend Medjugorje, or to show short-comings of spirituality; but, to add a balance that may possibly aid the reader and hopefully the writer in the development of spiritual living.

It would be wonderful if we could claim that everyone who reads about or visits Medjugorje is convinced that this is a gift from God. But that isn't the case. There are skeptics and opponents of the apparitions.

Much of the skepticism of anything smacking of the mystical or the miraculous comes because we Christians continue to divide the Church of Jesus Christ into hundreds of self-serving entities, each with its own set of spiritual rules. There is open rebellion to church authority of virtually every kind. In all denominations. The division within each denomination creates more divisions.

Even within the Medjugorje movement, there is division among groups based in the same area; thus we negate the basic message of individual peace, love and service to one another that Mary Virgin has come daily for so many years to this little village to teach us. Just as Jesus labored through three years of frustrating ministry, teaching the love of God, the Father, and love of one another, so Our Lady has labored in these ten years of grace.

That is perhaps why she repeats the basics of the message so many times. She is like our own concerned, loving mothers telling us over and over to be sure to wipe our shoes before coming into the house, or pick up our clothes and straighten our rooms.

At Medjugorje, she is a desperate mother standing in a burning house, repeating over and over instructions to her little ones on how to escape the imminent danger. But because it is Mary who has come to give these instructions and not Jesus Himself, she is rejected by many who do not understand her role.

Mary's love for us overrides the rejection she receives from so many faiths outside of the Catholic Church. Through the messages she continues to tell us that she is the Spiritual Mother of us all. She makes clear that she cannot perform miracles—only her Son, Jesus, can do that. She asks that we pray to Him, and she intercedes for us, as our mother.

Our mother from heaven is not without detractors in the Catholic Church, as well. One well-known priest told me that he thought there were too many followers of Mary who were overzealous; their demonstrative love of her shut out Jesus. It is as if they think Jesus could be jealous of His mother—difficult to imagine, when He sent her, and she constantly points us to Him.

I personally believe—and I feel that in the messages, Mary has confirmed —that Jesus gave Mary to us as our Spiritual Mother at the foot of the Cross. I cannot believe that a dying Jesus, hardly able to speak at all, took that particular time to assure only that His mother would be cared for in her earthly needs. Instead, I see Jesus giving Mary to us as our spiritual mother, and giving us to her as her children.

Unity is vital to living the message of Medjugorje. It is also vital for all of us who wish to be true followers of Christ, to live together in harmony. Regardless of how we become involved with Jesus and become followers, our role is to evangelize our brothers and sisters through the special grace from God by living the Gospel. The same applies to the messages given us at Medjugorje: they must be lived and understood in the light of their intent.

How do we do this? Mary has the answer in her messages at Medjugorje, just as she did at the wedding feast: "Do as my Son tells you."

"I am your mother and I warn you this time is a time of temptation. Satan is trying to find emptiness in you so he can enter and destroy you. Do not surrender! I pray with you. Do not pray

just with your lips, but pray with the heart. In this way prayer will obtain victory!"—July 4, 1988

Dear Mr. Weible:

I have just concluded reading most of your book, "Medjugorje: The Message." It is an interesting book. As you probably know, the Shrine at Lourdes of France has diminished to almost extinction, and I am wondering if the same thing will happen to Medjugorje in time.

There is the mystical element in religion, and it is impossible to rationalize, but I do know our God honors faith even though it is mixed with scriptural error. This is my explanation for Lourdes, and it is my explanation for Medjugorje.

Your writing has practically no reference to Holy Scripture. The doctrine of Mary was not a doctrine of the apostles or the Church Fathers. It was a later development. This is the problem I have with the overall thesis of your book. One who has a high view of the inerrant inspiration of Holy Scripture would have difficulty in all that you present. Those whose faith is based on tradition would have no difficulty with your thesis.

I praise God for the Charismatic Movement in the Roman Catholic Church. It needs, however, a cleansing purification of Bible truth. That does not take place over night. It is a slow process.

In Luke's nativity account, Mary, the mother of Christ, presents herself as a handmaiden, not Queen of Heaven, not one bodily assumed into Heaven and placed on the same level as our triune God. Study the scriptures and then read the creeds of the Christian faith, and this will not square with the view you present of God's handmaiden, Mary.

The Lord bless you.

Cordially yours in Christ,
Rev. Donald

Illinois

Dear Reverend Donald,

Thank you for your thoughtful letter. I am especially thankful that as a Christian brother, your criticism is without rancor.

First, regarding Lourdes, contrary to your belief, millions continue to pour into that Marian Shrine—with the same resultant conversion that occurs in Medjugorje. Incidentally, millions also continue to go to Fatima, in Portugal, and to Guadalupe, in Mexico, two other shrines where Mary appeared in apparition.

You say that the Christian faith is based solely on Holy Scripture. Where did Scripture come from, if not from tradition? As St Paul wrote in his second letter to the believers in Thessalonica, "*Therefore, brothers, stand firm. Hold fast to the traditions you received from us, either by our word or by letter.*" [II Thes. 2:15]

Your real problem with the apparitions of Medjugorje appears to be that Mary is the one sent to be the messenger. You do not see her as having a role beyond being the mother of Jesus and then returning to normal life. She was in the Upper Room with the other Apostles on the Day of Pentecost, and throughout the tradition of the early Church she has had a unique role. I do not see her as a divinity; rather, she has been given the role as Spiritual Mother, given to us by Christ from the Cross, a mother that always leads us to Him.

She was—and continues to be—the foremost of all God's prophets. And now she is His last.

The real issue, I suspect, is that you do not believe that Jesus is performing miracles today, as He performed them during His ministry. But we have miracles occurring around us every day. My miracle is that through Mary, I found Jesus. I found Him as a Protestant who had been passively anti-Catholic. I found that opening my heart to the real Gospel message of Jesus, that is living love, I no longer had time or desire to debate finite points that separate us as children of God.

But I sense that you love God as I do, and pray that love will unite us in His Spirit.

In Christ,
Wayne

"Those who are not Catholics, are no less creatures made in the image of God, and destined to rejoin someday, the House of the Father. Salvation is available to everyone, without exception. Only those who refuse God deliberately are condemned. To him who has been given little, little will be asked for. To whomever has been given much, very much will be required. It is God alone, in His infinite justice, who determines the degree of responsibility and pronounces judgment."—January 2, 1984

My dear brother in Christ Jesus, our Lord,

Jesus said to go forth to proclaim the Good News. That is in John 3:16 "For God so loved the world that He gave His only-begotten Son, so that whoever believes in Him shall not perish but have everlasting life." Are you proclaiming the Good News? Are you leading people to God? Or, are you taking people's eyes off the Almighty and leading them to love and adore Mary?

The first of the ten commandments in Exodus 20:3 "You shall have no other Gods besides Me." Are there statues of Mary at Medjugorje? Do the devoted bow down and pray before them? The answer is "yes."

The second of the commandments in Exodus 20:3 "You shall not make yourself any graven image of anything that is in the heavens above or that is in the earth beneath or that is in the water under the earth." That pretty much covers images, although there are thousands of scriptures that tell how an image is an abomination before God.

Oh, no. God only meant statues of calves, etc. Well, let's read in the New Testament in Romans 1:21 "Because when they knew and recognized Him as God, they did not honor and glorify Him as God or give thanks but became vain in their reasonings, and their senseless minds have been darkened. (22) For while professing to be wise, they have become fools (23) and they have changed the glory of the incorruptible God for an image made like to corruptible man, etc." Isn't God's word amazing? As is written in Hebrews 13:8 "Jesus Christ is the same yesterday, today and forever." God doesn't change; God still hates statues before Him.

Luke 11:27,28 "A woman from the crowd raised her voice and said, 'Blessed is the womb that bore you and the breast that nursed you'. Jesus said, 'More than that, blessed are those who hear the Word of God and keep it.' " Are you keeping the Word of God? Are you obeying His Word? The same scripture is verified in Mark 3:31.

I have quoted the first two (of the) Ten Commandments, and in Matthew 5:19, Jesus said, "Whoever then breaks or does away with or relaxes one of the least important of these commandments and teaches men so, shall be called least important in the Kingdom of heaven. Jesus called Himself (John 13:13) teacher and Lord. Is Jesus your teacher? Do you read your Bible everyday? Or, do you take time to say the rosary everyday? Do you find yourself becoming more devoted to Mary then to Jesus?

. . . 2 Corinthians 11:14 "The devil comes as an angel of light." Can you see how the Word tells all? In Revelation 19:10, John knelt to an angel and the angel said, "Do not do this, I am just another servant of Almighty God like yourself." Does this vision say do not kneel to me for I am just another servant of Almighty God? In Luke 1:38 "Then Mary said, behold, I am the hand-maiden of the Lord." Mary knew she was God's servant.

You write (that) the children say there are signs to come but Jesus said in Matthew 24:23,24 "If anyone says to you then, lo, here is Christ, the Messiah! or, there He is! Do not believe it! For false Christs and false prophets will arise, and they will show great signs and wonders, so as to deceive and lead astray, even the elect." Do these beautiful children know scripture? Do they know the devil wants to lead astray even the elect?

The Lord Jesus tells us false Christs and false prophets will show great signs. Matthew 24:25 "See, I have warned you before hand." These are the words of Jesus, not mine. Jesus tells us all before it happens. He is an awesome God. Also

Revelation 16:14 tells us about the end of the world, saying "spirits and demons performing signs." In Matthew 12:39, Jesus answered, "An evil and adulterous generation seeks after a sign. . . ."

Again, I warn you do not be as the teachers in Luke 11:52 "Woe to you teachers! For you have taken away the key of knowledge." The key of knowledge is the Word of God. . . THE BIBLE!

Your sister in Christ Jesus our Lord,
Mary Ellen

New York

Dear Mary Ellen,

I thank you for taking the time to write to me and to look up all of that Scripture to make your point. However, you could have saved yourself a lot of time and energy, if you had only been able to see the confirmation of Medjugorje in all that you quote. Its message is the Gospel message renewed.

Mary Ellen, do you have any pictures of your family hanging in your home? Are they graven images? Do you "worship" them, or—as with all of us—do they serve as reminders of loved ones?

To answer your first question, yes, I do feel that I am attempting to lead people to Jesus Christ. That is the basic message of Medjugorje. My interpretation of what God gives us in Scripture possibly varies a bit from yours, but I do not fault you for that; I simply try to fulfill what I feel is His mission for me.

Your knowledge of Mary seems limited to that taught in your nondenominational church. You quote Scripture to make your point, but can you show me in Scripture where it says we are to split into thousands of different churches with thousands of different interpretations of Scripture?

Do you know how to determine if such events as Medjugorje are really Satan disguised as an angel of light? If I might now quote you one long piece of Scripture that might help you understand a little more about events like Medjugorje: "Then a member of the Sanhedrin stood up, a Pharisee named Gamaliel, a teacher of the law highly regarded by all the people. He had the accused ordered out of court for a few minutes, and then said to the assembly, 'Fellow Israelites, think twice about what you are going to do with these men. Not long ago a certain Theudas came on the scene and tried to pass himself off as someone of importance. About four hundred men joined him. However he was killed, and all those who had been so easily convinced by him were disbanded. In the end it came to nothing. Next came Judas the Galilean at the time of the census. He too built up quite a following, but likewise died, and all his followers were dispersed. The present case is similar. My advice is that you have nothing to do with these men. Let them alone. If their purpose or activity is human in its origins, it will destroy itself. If, on the other hand, it comes from God, you will not be able to destroy them without fighting God himself.' " [Acts 5:34-39]

Forgive me for this rather long quotation, but I think it makes the point. I will pray that in the future you will judge a tree by its fruit. Note that the good fruit of Medjugorje has been occurring for ten years now. And it continues to lead people to Christ Jesus.

May we pray for one another that we may indeed do Christ's will.

> In Christ,
> Wayne

"I wish to engrave in every heart the sign of love. If you love all mankind, then there is peace in you. If you are at peace with all men, it is the kingdom of love."—January 18, 1984

Dear Editor (sent to our office)

The Protestant lay speaker, Mr. Wayne Weible, has exerted efforts to arouse belief in the highly publicized claims of Marian apparitions in the place of Medjugorje, Yugoslavia. Mr. Weible's efforts have been permitted by Catholics in a vague hope that he may succeed in bringing back to the Catholic faith at least a minority of the tens of millions of Catholic faithful who have been spiritually and emotionally separated by a severe crisis of the faith, which has occurred during the post-Vatican II period.

The most Holy Virgin Mary, Our Lady of the Apocalypse at Fatima, came in the year 1917, and in successive visits to Sister Lucia afterwards to reveal this crisis, and to provide the one heaven-sent remedy to prevent it. God has certified the message and the remedy of our Lady of Fatima as coming from Him. The Fatima miracles of the convulsions of the sun with the testimony of 70,000 witnesses gravely oblige us to believe and to obey the message. On that terrible day of October 13, people swooned with fear at the trepidations of the sun. They confessed their sins out loud. Many were indisputably cured of diseases and incurable illnesses in an instant at the same time as the miracle of the sun by Our Lady of the Apocalypse at Fatima.

Our Lady of Fatima stated the necessity of penance, and of the daily praying of the rosary, wearing the brown scapular, and the formal institution of the preparatory devotion of the first five Saturdays, and most importantly, She stated the necessity of the consecration of Russia to the Immaculate Heart of Mary, and stated that She would return to again make this request. The fulfillment of Her promise to return came to Sister Lucia in the apparition of June 13, 1929, at Tuy (Portugal) when Our Lady declared, "The moment has come in which God asks the Holy Father in union with all the bishops of the world, to consecrate Russia to my Immaculate Heart, promising to save it by this means."

Needless to say, the enemy of God, Satan, has opposed this act of consecration which will end the crisis of faith in the Holy Church, convert Russia, which is the seat of Satanic Communism, and end the horrible scourges of abortion, apostasy, and the plague. Satan has opposed this one act with all the fury of hell. . . .

Now, five years have passed since Dr. Weible heard this locution from this spirit of the apparition of Medjugorje, telling him to devote his life to spread its message of a world religion which is neither Catholic nor Protestant. This spirit of this apparition of Medjugorje is by its own admission not Catholic. In numerous depositions it equivocates all religions as being acceptable to God and equal to the one true, holy faith, and therefore, cannot be divine.

The Immaculate Conception is the Rock upon which all heresies against the faith are broken. Only the Holy Catholic Faith upholds this truth. All man-made sects and religions betray themselves by denying it. The Holy Virgin is the indestructible rampart of truth in God's holy church. He has set Her as a sign and clothed Her with the sun. "Behold thy Mother!"

The apparitions of Medjugorje have been lawfully and justly condemned by the true ecclesiastical authorities of that region. We must listen to Christ in His Church. They were duly condemned due to heresies propagated by errors against the True Faith. Anyone who pays devotion to this wayward spirit does so at grave risk to his soul. Divination is rebellion, and presumption is idolatry.

It is obvious fact that the Communists have fully cooperated in the promotion of these Medjugorje apparitions which evangelize for a one-world religion and effectively promote the New World order, so desired by Bush and Gorbachev. They eagerly support the development of the false, one world religion in order to contribute to the destruction of the one, Holy Catholic Faith, which is the only opposition feared by the Communists, and the only opponent capable of their defeat. They know only too well that when the earth is a free republic ruled by the will of men, the Antichrist will be on his throne.

If Dr. Weible is a man of goodwill and he truly wishes to love and to honor the Mother of God, he must renounce Luther who renounces Her; he must embrace the Holy Catholic Faith, and profess without reservation all the infallible doctrines of the Holy, Catholic, Apostolic Church. Until that time, all his efforts and admonitions to "conversion" must be held in contempt by the faithful

Catholic people. Before he can convert others, he must convert himself.

> In God and
> His Most Holy Virgin Mother,
> Mary's child (unsigned)

Letter writers such as the one above, while very sincere and positive about the Blessed Virgin Mary and apparitions, lose sight as so many do of a major truth: we are judged by God, by our acceptance, our actions, and our sincerity in attempting to follow His laws.

How many times I have been subjected to criticism by those who feel they have the whole truth while others do not. Certainly the apparitions of Fatima in 1917 are important. But the Lady of Medjugorje is the *same* Lady who came to Fatima. And to Lourdes and Guadeloupe and so many other sites throughout history. And the purpose of her coming to Medjugorje, like the other holy areas, is the same.

Whenever I am confronted with skeptics of Medjugorje's message who become accusing or judgmental in their critiques, I think of the story of Lazarus in the Gospel of John, particularly: *Jesus began to weep, which caused the Jews to remark, "See how much He loved him!"* [John ll:35-36]

Jesus wept for several reasons; first, the awesome magnitude of the miracle that the Father was about to give to mankind, the resurrection of Lazarus from the grave after four days of putrefaction of the flesh; second, the inspiring lesson for His disciples, a lesson of God's performance of the impossible that would buoy them in the establishment of His Church after His ascent into heaven; and third, out of agony that the Scribes and Pharisees would not be converted by this miracle. On the contrary, they would hate Him even more and would pursue His demise with greater vigor.

Thus, I pray that the good fruits of Medjugorje may eventually unite us who love God, that we would put aside our differences and become one family for Him. For I see the miracle of Medjugorje to be of the same magnitude as that of the raising of Lazarus.

"My Son suffers very much because men do not want to be reconciled. They have not listened to me. Be converted, be reconciled."—September 26, 1983

Make every effort to preserve the unity which has the Spirit as its origin and peace as its binding force. There is but one body and one Spirit, just as there is but one hope given all of you by your call. There is one Lord, one faith, one baptism, one God and Father of all, who is over all, and works through all, and is in all." [Ephes. 4:3-6]

12

Signs, Kisses from Heaven

"The wind is my sign. I will come in the wind. When the wind blows, know that I am with you. You have learned that the cross represents Christ; it is a sign of Him. It is the same for the crucifix you have in your home. For me, it is not the same. When it is cold, you come to church; you want to offer everything to God. I am then with you. I am with you in the wind. Do not be afraid."—February 15, 1984

How well I remember on my first trip to Medjugorje in May, 1986, when our group was unexpectedly invited along with other pilgrims to go up on the hill where Our Lady had first appeared, for a special Monday evening apparition. For me, it was an opportunity to be present when the Mother of God visited with the visionaries. All kinds of fantasies ran through my mind. Would I be privileged to see Mary as they did? How I longed for that, as I am sure many others have as well.

As it turned out, I didn't see Mary. Neither did anyone else, other than the visionaries, though many claimed to see mysterious lights and other unusual things. But all of us experienced a special sign as we came down from the little hill: birds were singing with all their might—and it was midnight!

As we boarded our bus for the short drive back to Citluk where we were staying, one large lady sat down, heaved a deep sigh and said, "I'm so disappointed, I didn't see a thing!"

I couldn't believe it. Here we had been given the special blessing of being present during an apparition, and she was disappointed because she didn't see any special phenomena.

We all want signs from heaven confirming that what is happening at Medjugorje is really from God. *We* want to see Mary, just as the visionaries see her. Is there one of us who has become involved with Medjugorje who has not prayed for this?

One evening I was praying about the signs, hoping that certain people I wanted converted would see many signs and wonders at Medjugorje. Suddenly, as though Our Lady was speaking directly to my heart, I discerned that the *real* signs and wonders pertaining to Medjugorje's apparitions are the thousands upon thousands of spiritual conversions. It is an obvious example of the old cliche: we can't see the forest for the trees.

The popular signs of Mary Virgin's presence at the little village are rosary chains turning to gold and the phenomena of the dancing, spinning sun. Old rosaries and new rosaries alike suddenly have their metal chains change from a silver to a gold color; I have also seen gold-colored rosaries turn silver—and then back to gold again. The sun is seen dancing and spinning and throwing off a rainbow of colors; images that stay a few moments and then fade are often seen as well. The cross on Mount Krizevac that dominates the valley, has been seen to totally disappear; or to turn slowly in place.

What does it all mean? According to the visionaries,

Our Lady has confirmed many of these signs and has told them that they are small confirmations for the unbelievers. We might say that they are "kisses from heaven."

The few letters I receive concerning signs are usually about a photograph that was supposedly taken at Medjugorje during the time of the apparition, or on the hill where Mary first appeared. They seem to have an image of Mary mysteriously appear somewhere in them. Unfortunately, many of them are not authentic. Others might be. Regardless of authenticity, though, they serve a purpose.

I remember in the first days of learning about Medjugorje, I saw such a picture that the owner claimed was taken at Medjugorje. It showed the Blessed Mother with the baby Jesus in her arms, surrounded by a halo of light. It was beautiful. Later, I discovered that it was actually a painting taken from an Italian Christmas card.

For me this picture came to represent my image of Mary at Medjugorje. I framed it and placed it in a conspicuous spot where I could see it every day. I really didn't worry whether it was real or not; it simply served for me as do many of these small signs and wonders, a reminder that God indeed is with us in miracles today, the same as He was nearly 2,000 years ago.

"Hurry to be converted. Do not wait for the great sign. For the unbelievers, it will then be too late to be converted. For you who have the faith, this time constitutes a great opportunity for you to be converted, and to deepen your faith."—December, 1982

Dear Wayne,

I just finished reading your book and I want to tell you about a happening I experienced in Medjugorje.

I was born the youngest of nine children in mixed faiths of Baptist and Catholic. I attended public school in the first grade then transferred to Catholic school and was taught by a very strict group of Franciscan nuns and priests. I became an altar boy and assisted at Mass for four or five years and loved it.

I graduated and joined the Navy in 1951, and this is when I began to drift away from the Church and did not practice my religion for twenty-five years. I married at age 28 and had two children. My daughter became intolerable, and addicted to drugs at the age of 14. I could not handle this situation by myself, so after two years of hell, I went to a priest and was given absolution.

I have been back in the church and receiving the sacraments for the last eleven years and have been able to cope with my daughter's addiction in a much better fashion.

I heard about Medjugorje in 1988, and knew I had to go and pray for my daughter's recovery and my own. I made arrangements to go March, 1990, and now I will tell you what happened on the early morning of the 19th, the day before we were to leave for Dubrovnik and fly home the next day.

I awoke at 5:00 AM, with a very dry and parched mouth and had to go to the bathroom sink to get a drink of water. When I went back to get in bed, I looked out the window which faced

Apparition Hill (where The Blessed Virgin first appeared) and saw nothing but pitch black. Then, the sky turned into millions of small, very white fluffy clouds with a light cast of blue in the background. I stared at this dumb-founded, for about sixty seconds, and then everything turned dark again.

I remember you saying in one of the passages in your book why the Blessed Mother gives signs to people of ordinary lives. All I know is that my life has been changed, and I have never had as much peace in my life as I do now. It is a peace that passes all understanding. My sign will stay with me for the rest of my life.

> Peace be with you,
> Jim

Ohio

"My dear children, for this year I want to tell you, pray! Your mother loves you. I want to collaborate with you for I need your collaboration. I want you to become, dear children, my announcers and my sons who will bring peace, love, conversion. . . I want you to be a sign for others. In this new year I want to give you peace, I want to give you love and harmony. Abandon all your problems and all your difficulties to me. Live my messages. Pray, pray!"—January 2, 1989

I had spoken on a cold evening in Cheyenne, Wyoming, about the wonderful power of healing that is given us by Jesus, through the Holy Spirit. I had quoted the beautiful Scripture verse: "I solemnly assure you, the man who has faith in me will do the works I do, and greater far than these." [John 14:12] I used it to make the point that we can heal with the same hands that have sinned when we truly believe. At the close of the talk those in spiritual and physical pain had spontaneously come forward to be healed.

This awesome gift was a special sign for me of God's presence during my ongoing learning conversion stemming from Medjugorje. And as had happened before, it was being called on for this evening's witness. That is not to say that I have the gift of healing at my beck and call. But I learned through prayer, fasting and listening, that it is called on by the Holy Spirit at certain times, and this was one of those times.

After awhile, a young man approached me. I had noticed him earlier, hanging near the people who had come forward to be prayed over. But he had stayed his distance. Now he was standing in front of me, shaking all over and looking down at the floor. "Mr. Weible, I need you to pray over me—I'm addicted to marijuana—I need help, please, would you pray over me so I can stop?"

I placed my hands on him and prayed as hard as I could for a healing of this addiction that captures so many young people. I also prayed for others who suffered the same addiction, having learned that when we pray for certain intentions for individuals, we should also pray for all who are in need of the same healing or help. Then I gave him a medal from Medjugorje and told him that every time he felt the urge to smoke marijuana, to place the medal in his hands and pray for the strength to reject it.

"But I have the stuff at home! I'm afraid I'll smoke it as long as it's in the house!"

"Listen, even if you fail the first time and the second time—or even a third time, don't stop! Use the medal to remind you of God's love; ask His forgiveness each

time you slip, but have faith that you will be healed!"
I added that I would continue to pray for him.

Several weeks later we received a telephone call at the
office. It was the young man from Wyoming. He was
jubilant; he had finally been healed of the marijuana habit.
It was his sign—and mine—that the words of Mary
concerning the power of prayer being able to alter the
laws of nature, were true.

*"I wish to engrave in every heart the sign of love. If you love
all mankind, then there is peace in you. If you are at peace
with all men, it is the kingdom of love."—January 18, 1984*

Dear Mr. Weible,
   One year ago I was visiting my parents in
Emerald Isle, when my mother showed me your
original columns on Medjugorje. Considering
myself "college educated," I read your articles
with apprehension and skepticism. However,
sparked with curiosity, I agreed to accompany my
mom to one of your speaking engagements.
   After your talk, I purchased your book and
while you were autographing it, you reached into
your pocket and handed me a Medjugorje medal.
You told me that you did not hand out these
medals randomly, but only gave them to those
selected by the Blessed Mother.
   As I walked out of the church, still clutching the
medal in my hand, I told my mother what had
transpired. Tears came to her eyes. When I told
her that she was the one who deserved the medal
(you see, she's been spiritually faithful, attending

Mass, praying the rosary, etc. all her life, not I) she responded, "No, you're the skeptic." She said that I needed the reminder. She was so right!

Since that day last March, the message of Medjugorje has stayed on my mind and in my heart. I am now attending Mass again, and even serve as a Eucharistic minister in my church. My faith in God is much stronger and my life finally feels complete.

In two weeks, thanks to my supportive husband and my loving parents, I will be making my first pilgrimage, destination: Medjugorje! I'm not sure why I've longed to go since last year, but there's been a feeling in my heart that makes me believe that I'm being called by the Holy Spirit. This feeling was reinforced when your March newsletter came today. Within the printed context were two very special messages. The first was yours: "Go to Medjugorje!" The second from the Blessed Mother, "I am blessing each of you and each good decision of yours. . .".

So, Mr. Weible, I owe you a thank you for reawakening me through the message of Medjugorje. Thank you for responding to Her call.

Sincerely,
Gina

North Carolina

"This is a time for grace. That is why I would like you to pray as much as you can during this time. Especially, I would like you to renew the family prayer!"—November 7, 1988

Dear Mr. Weible,

I'll try to make this brief, but I've got a lot to say.

About three years ago you to came to Cleveland to speak, and I drove from a suburb to hear you. After your talk I spoke to you for about a minute or two and you did a wonderful thing for me— you gave me one of three little medals you had in your pocket. You said, "Something tells me to give you one of these medals blessed by Mary at Medjugorje."

I gave that medal to my husband who, raised as an Episcopalian, was a self-professed agnostic. Although he attended Mass with me and agreed to bring our children up Catholic, he really never embraced any religion.

Anyway, he carried that medal with him always until one day he couldn't find it. After several months and a prayer by me specifically to our Lord in the Blessed Sacrament, it turned up mysteriously on our kitchen counter, which had been cleared and cleaned a million times without any sign of the medal.

He has since worn it around his neck and he just read your book while on a business trip to Las Vegas. He called me the next morning from there and said he had said the rosary that morning!

So I thank the Blessed Virgin and our Lord for the graces my husband is receiving and responding to, and I thank you for your role and the kindness you showed me three years ago.

Sincerely,
Sarah

Ohio

P.S. I made my first visit to Medjugorje last month and I have been so homesick for that place since coming home!

"I am with you even if you are not conscious of it. I want to protect you from everything that Satan offers you, and through which he wants to destroy you. As I bore Jesus in my womb, so also, dear children, do I wish to bear you unto holiness. God wants to save you and sends you messages through men, nature, and so many things which can only help you to understand that you must change the direction of your life. Therefore, little children, understand also the greatness of the gift which God is giving you through me, so that I may protect you with my mantle and lead you to the joy of life."—March 25, 1990

I will pour out my spirit upon all mankind. Your sons and daughters shall prophesy, your old men shall dream dreams, your young men shall see visions; even upon the servants and the handmaids, in those days, I will pour out my spirit. And I will work wonders in the heavens and on the earth, blood, fire, and columns of smoke. [Joel 2:28-30]

13

The Grace of Healing

"Dear children, for these days while you are joyfully celebrating the Cross, I desire that your cross also would be a joy for you. Especially, dear children, pray that you may be able to accept sickness and suffering with love the way Jesus accepted them. Only that way shall I be able with joy to give out to you the graces and healing which Jesus is permitting me."—September 11, 1986.

How do we accept a cross with joy? What parent can truly say that the suffering of their child can be seen as a grace? How difficult for us to understand this message of healing without fully understanding the gift of redemptive suffering given us by Jesus. It is the ultimate gift.

Through the messages she brings to us at Medjugorje, Mary Virgin teaches us to accept this ultimate gift. She asks us to give complete surrender to God and to accept with joy our crosses. This is true healing; for the soul must be healed first in order to believe in the power of prayer and fasting for physical healing.

There is the story I told in my first book of a young Croatian woman who had drifted away from her faith through marriage to a man actively involved in the Communist Party. She no longer called on God for her needs.

When her first child was born crippled with a form of muscular dystrophy, she had no one to turn to for help other than herself. In the ensuing five years this tragedy plus increasing pressures of life took a fearful toll on her. She began to suffer from acute anxiety, for which she took medication in ever larger doses. Eventually this developed into epilepsy. The frequency and severity of her seizures progressed to the point where she was hospitalized. As a result of radical medical treatment, she went blind.

Now this young mother, already burdened with a suffering child confined to a wheel chair, became an invalid herself and could only await the finality of death.

Somewhere during that time an extraordinary thing happened. She began to hear an inner message: "You must turn to God and pray." Did she dare ask this loving God whom she had depended on most of her life to forgive her and to listen to her now?

The woman's husband concluded that she was delirious from her illness when she confided in him about the message. She insisted the voice was asking her to go outside, and of course, the husband refused to let his sick wife leave her bed.

Eventually, she was left alone long enough to crawl outside to the yard. No sooner had she made it than she suddenly was blessed with an apparition of the Blessed Virgin Mary. Ever the mother first, she thought of her crippled five-year-old son and pleaded with Our Lady, "Please, Blessed Mary, please heal my son!"

Mary Virgin's answer was startling: *"Your son is not responsible for his affliction, but his suffering will be the salvation and conversion of many people. Do not ask for him; ask for yourself. Come to Medjugorje and you will be healed."*

After much convincing argument with her husband, the woman was able to go to Medjugorje and was indeed healed. And so was her husband spiritually. But her son was not healed. He continues his redemptive suffering.

How do you tell parents that the suffering of their child serves for the salvation of others? You can't; they must discover for themselves, through faith and unceasing prayers, that these tragedies can change from burden to blessing with full acceptance of God's will.

This does not mean we can't continue to pray for physical healing. We continue to ask God for His mercy, and as a result, there are thousands of medically unexplainable miracles. This Croatian woman is more than likely still asking that her son be healed; but she has accepted it as a blessing now. It has led to transformation of her family from the emptiness of living without God to the daily blessings of grace He gives us when we abide by His will.

"For the cure of the sick, it is important to say the following prayers: the Creed, and seven times each, the Lord's Prayer, the Hail Mary, and the Glory Be; and, to fast on bread and water."—July 25, 1982

In March, 1988, Kent Kimball, Jr. was shaking hands and having his picture taken with the visionaries in Medjugorje. He and his family were deeply touched by Mary Virgin's apparitions. It changed the lives of this Memphis, Tennessee family, adding to an already good family life the gifts of fasting, family prayer and complete surrender to God.

In the Spring of 1989, Kent, a promising fourteen-year-old athlete, was taken to the doctor because of pain in his right knee. He and his family were shocked to learn that he had a malignant tumor in his right leg.

The tumor was removed in July, and he was given an artificial knee implant. Kent's athletic days were over. Chemotherapy was begun at that time at St Jude's Children's Hospital in Memphis, and Kent continues to spend much of his time in the hospital, struggling with the treatments and physical therapy.

Throughout the ordeal Kent and his family have been able to accept this cross because of their faith in God—a faith that was steeled by their trip to Medjugorje. They have accepted God's will in their lives, and God has made Kent a very special messenger.

In November, 1989, President George Bush visited Memphis and toured St Jude's children's ward. Kent was one of the children privileged to meet the President. They talked of Kent's hopes of attending Notre Dame someday, and the President wished him luck. His few moments with the President apparently over, Kent sat down.

But he was not finished. He had a mission, and he knew what had to be done. A few minutes later, with the eyes of the press and all cameras on him, Kent limped over to President Bush, and excusing himself for the interruption, handed the President two medals from Medjugorje, which had been blessed by Our Lady. President Bush then asked him what they were, and of course, Kent told him about the miracle of Medjugorje.

For this young man, the actual meeting of the President wasn't nearly as important as the opportunity and joy in being able to tell the world's most powerful leader about Medjugorje, and Mary's messages of peace. While he still suffers from his physical illness, Kent has indeed been healed.

"My angels, I send you my Son, Jesus, who was tortured for His faith, and yet He endured everything. You also, my angels, will endure everything."—July 27, 1981

Dear Mr. Weible,

I feel compelled to write to you and tell you about a miracle that has happened in our family through the grace of Our Lady at Medjugorje.

In September, 1989, you spoke at our church about Medjugorje. Some close friends of ours were there, and afterwards they felt they should speak to you about our eight-year-old son, Adam. He has been suffering from cancer for three years. That evening, you gave our friends a special medal that was blessed by Our lady at Medjugorje, and told them that Mary chose who you were to give it to, not you; and, she chose that Adam should have one.

On the next Sunday, we met our friends in a park for our children to get together and have a play. They passed the medal on to me. On Monday, Adam had to be admitted to the hospital for his third major operation in two years. In 1987, he lost his kidney to cancer, but only 95% of the tumor was dead when they removed it. In April, 1988, he relapsed and lost half his lung, and again, only 95% of the tumor was dead when removed.

A year later, Adam relapsed again. We were told this was very serious. The tumor was inoperable and it took us several months of chemotherapy to try and reduce it. In that time we almost lost Adam many times. His little system was having a lot of trouble coping with the drugs and the tumor at the same time. Finally in September, we found a surgeon who would agree to do the surgery.

So, the morning before the surgery, I placed Our Lady's medal on Adam and told him that Mary was going to go inside him and make everything all right. He accepted that and off we went to the hospital. Adam's operation had been scheduled to be last on the surgeon's list because it was the longest. They weren't sure when he would go to the operating theater.

I felt extremely upset that we would have to wait maybe all day. But Mary was listening and when my husband and I walked into the hospital ward at 8:00 AM, we were met by the nurse who said the surgeon was going to take Adam first.

Naturally, Adam is always very agitated before surgery, as we all are, but that day he was extremely calm and told us not to worry, that everything was going to be all right.

The surgeon spoke to us before he took Adam to the theater, telling us he didn't know how long it would be, maybe all day. He stated they did not know where the tumor was coming from, but thought it was the abdomen, but extending off the base of the lung. He was an abdomen specialist and said he might have to call in a thoracic surgeon if need be.

Seven and a half hours later, they wheeled Adam to intensive care and told us he was extremely weak; the next two-three days would tell. He lost his spleen to the tumor, but it was coming from his diaphragm, which was most unusual.

All the time Adam was in surgery, I held his Medjugorje medal and prayed to Mary. I was calm. All I said was it's Mary doing. Half of the people there who noticed my calmness and heard me didn't know what I was saying. The next day, Adam had recovered enough to be taken to the general ward. We were thrilled! Again, Mary was working with us.

Three days later at 6:00 PM, I got a phone call from our specialist. I went weak at the knees and felt sick. He told me he was ringing with news from the pathology lab, and that it was good. The whole tumor was dead and that Adam could recover completely before doing any radiotherapy. That was our miracle; in three tumors (before), there had never been total cell kill.

Adam is really well at the moment. He has been attending school and won a gold medal last week for tennis at school. He lives life to the fullest and enjoys every day of his life and health.

We had a cat scan done last week and a nodule showed up where his spleen was. I panicked, but in a test done the following day, the nodule turned out to be a small spleen that is functioning! It has either regrown a bit like tonsils, or was missed at surgery.

I'm sorry I've been a bit long-winded about this story but a miracle has been given to us through Adam and last Wednesday, the doctor said that Adam is a walking miracle to recover and be as good as he is with what his body has been through. We still have a long way to go, but our faith and belief in Mary's intercession is very strong. We hope and pray everyday for continued health for all the children in the ward where he was infirmed.

Our blessings on you and your family. I hope you continue to do your good work.

Kind regards,
Lorraine

Australia

In 1983, when the Blessed Mother was asked to cure someone, she explained: *"I cannot cure. God alone cures. Pray! I will pray with you. Believe firmly. Fast, do penance. I will help you, as long as it is in my power to do it. God comes to help everyone. I am not God. I need your sacrifices and your prayers to help me."*

On a trip to Great Britain in 1990, I met a little girl in Wales named Geraldine who had cancer and wasn't expected to live much longer. She also had one of the most beautiful smiles I had ever seen and a warm, happy personality to match.

I met this little eight-year-old and the rest of her family rather unexpectedly. While at the home of my host family, as we were finishing our evening meal prior to leaving for my talk, the woman mentioned Geraldine and her disease. "Would you please offer a special prayer for her healing, and for her family?" She gripped my hand, and her eyes moistened as she made the request. "She is a lovely, happy child, and her family has been through so much."

I assured her I would pray for this little girl and her family, and then I asked, "Will she by chance be at the talk tonight?" I was hoping to be able to actually pray over her and to give her a medal from Medjugorje.

"No—she isn't feeling too well and her father is keeping

her while her mother comes to hear you."

A thought suddenly entered my mind. "Could we possibly stop by to see her on the way to the auditorium?"

The woman lit up. Jumping to her feet she grabbed the telephone, spoke for a minute and hanging up, said, "Yes, we can stop by, but we must leave immediately. I'm afraid you won't have time for that cup of tea and dessert!"

Spoons clattered, and chairs were pushed back as we hastily piled into the waiting automobile which her husband had quickly pulled to the front of the house. Very shortly we were sitting with Geraldine and her father in her little living room.

It was a most rewarding twenty minutes. This bright and happy little girl was thrilled that I had actually come by to see her. She had just the evening before watched a video on Medjugorje, that included a few scenes of my witnessing.

How do you fall in love with someone in twenty minutes? Only by the grace of sharing God's love! With Geraldine, it was easy. She was very aware that she had a terrible sickness. But she remained cheerful and optimistic. She had had two operations for this cruel disease which she was first diagnosed as having at the age of four—half of her young life.

Geraldine was fortunate in another way: she had incredible parents. They were both filled with faith and acceptance of God's will. Knowing the cost of Geraldine's illness in time, money, and suffering, they had also adopted a two-year-old boy who is mentally retarded. They knew his condition when they adopted him.

I talked with Geraldine, gave her the medal, and then prayed over her—and her little adopted brother. Then it was time to leave.

After arriving back in the United States, I couldn't forget Geraldine. I knew she had to go to Medjugorje. I prayed for her physical healing because I knew that she and her family were already spiritually healed. Six months later Geraldine and her father did go to Medjugorje.

I had hoped to see her there and had even made plans to do so. Unfortunately, I would miss them by a day. When I learned this, I asked a large group of pilgrims during a talk behind the church to pray for this child to be healed when she arrived. I asked them to literally go up to her, lay hands on her and pray to the Holy Spirit for the gift of healing.

At last report, Geraldine is doing wonderfully, is back in school, and is playing again like any normal eight-year-old. Recently I received this letter from her aunt:

> Dear Wayne,
>
> Pat Loftus is my sister and you aided in sending Geraldine to Medjugorje. She is doing quite well now. The weather has been cold and she feels it badly and has lost some time from school, but she now has plenty of energy. I hope this is a good sign.
>
> Geraldine told me all about her visit to Medjugorje, and how she had felt a warmth going through her body when Vicka, the visionary, prayed over her.
>
> Thank you so much for your prayers for her.
>
> > Yours thankfully,
> > Agnes Christmas
>
> Wales

In August of 1982, when Mirjana asked how someone who is sick should pray, she was told: *"Have them believe and pray; I cannot help him who does not pray and does not sacrifice. The sick, just like those who are in good health, must pray and fast for the sick. The more you believe firmly, the more you pray and fast for the same intention, the greater is the grace and the mercy of God."*

Dear Wayne,

I met you in September, 1990, in Connecticut, at the Marian Retreat in Southington, for Mary's birthday (the 8th). I've never had such a moving experience. The woman who had gotten me the ticket unexpectedly went to you and explained how I was going for surgery for the removal of a six-inch dermoid on my ovary. You had given her a miraculous medal from Medjugorje to give to me.

At the end of the Mass, I went to personally thank you, and you said to keep it (the medal) with me always, and that it was from Mary. It carried me through a very successful surgery and a most speedy recovery.

I took it off my chain on December 17th, to replace it with an amethyst my husband gave me several Valentine Days ago, and probably never had worn. I pinned Mary's medal under my sweater. That night, I thought I returned it to the chain, went to bed, but noticed the next night it was gone. I have searched, prayed, searched, prayed; I cannot find it. I sort of feel punished for hiding it under my sweater, or placing the amethyst above it. I am very depressed. I guess I'm sort of hoping you will send me another even though I've been careless and proud. Also, I must tell you, this medal had never tarnished as the other Medjugorje medals have. May I hear from you?

Sincerely,
Carmel

Connecticut

Dear Carmel,

Please find enclosed a replacement medal for the one that you lost; I know how much it meant to you and I want to assure you that you were not being "punished" for replacing it with a jewel.

Carmel, you received the *spiritual value* of the medal with the successful operation and healing. It was your faith in God and the intercession of Our Lady that gave the medal its personal value to you. I pray that you will place the same value on this one I have enclosed.

Please know that I will keep you in my prayers, and I ask that you pray specifically for your friend who loved and cared enough to ask for the medal for you in the first place.

May Jesus and Mary always lead you to love your neighbor as this neighbor of yours has loved you.

In Christ,
Wayne

"Without faith, nothing is possible. All those who will believe firmly will be cured."—July 25, 1981

Dear Wayne,

My husband Gary and I were with the Peace Center tour you led in April (1990). I wanted to write concerning an event that took place our last night in Medjugorje.

Joel, a young man in our group shared with us during a sharing time, that he went over to the church and went to confession for the first time in ten years. He said that he had been somewhat lax in the practice of his faith, but did say the rosary from time to time. That night after dinner, Joe and some other young people got together to pray for physical healing for Joe and a beautiful young woman from our group, who I think was named Melissa. She was suffering with Multiple Sclerosis, and had come to Medjugorje with her father.

Joel's problem was significant. He had been in the army in Turkey, and was run over by a truck which did extensive damage to his legs. After two years in the hospital, his foot had been fused to his ankle and was permanently elevated from the floor. He had suffered from severe bone infections and doctors were still uncertain as to whether the leg could be saved.

The following morning, our group was "buzzing" about what had happened to Joel. The word was he had seen Jesus and his leg was healed and perfectly normal! On the airplane going home, my husband asked Joel what had happened; I hope I can repeat his story, as my husband told it to me.

He said five young people were praying for the young woman with MS. Joel was especially deep in prayer with his eyes closed and very much concentrating on asking for healing for Melissa. Suddenly, Our Lady put Her arms around Joel and Melissa; in front of them was Jesus. Around Him was a bright glow. Mary presented the two of them to Jesus. He smiled at them. At that moment, Joel said that he felt heat or a warmth go through his leg. He opened his eyes and his foot was loosened and flat on the floor! He was a very grateful, happy person the following day, but reluctant about spreading the news. I don't know

about Melissa; she did not seem to know if anything special happened to her.

Wayne, this is such a beautiful story. Is there
any way to follow-up and find out the rest of it?
Joel said he was going to have his leg x-rayed
immediately and I feel certain that Jesus was
there for Melissa, too. If you should hear anything further, could you let us know?

Thank you for the beautiful and inspiring talks
and for the witness of your devotion to Our Lady
and Jesus.

God bless you!
LaVerne

Wisconsin

Dear LaVerne,

Thank you for letting me know of the wonderful events
that occurred on our April trip. I thank God for all of
the individual miracles that happen to people when they
respond to Mary's call to come to Medjugorje.

There are thousands of such stories like that of Joel
and Melissa; there will be many more. The beautiful part
is that they will not be authenticated to assist in the
investigation of the events of Medjugorje; there are far
too many, and that in itself is an unofficial authentication.

The dramatic impact of Joel's foot being healed on the
other pilgrims on this trip will trigger many more mini-
miracles; most of them will be healing of the spirit. I feel
that is why Our Lady calls us there, so that Her Son Jesus
can pour out His mercy on us. It takes the drama of physical
healing in one child of God to bring about the spiritual
healing in many others.

As for Melissa, possibly her *physical healing* is ongoing;
I do know from conversations with her and her father

that the spirit was strong in both of them, and there was full acceptance of her handicap, regardless of what might develop for her in coming to Medjugorje. That, of course, is full submission to the will of the Father, which is the real reason there is a Medjugorje.

May Jesus and Mary continue to be with you, and may you continue to pray for all that were in our group.

In Christ,
Wayne

"Raise your hands and open your hearts. Now, at the time of the Resurrection, Jesus wishes to give you a special gift. This gift of my Son is my gift. Here it is. You will be subjected to trials and you will endure them with great ease. We will be ready to show you how to escape from them if you accept us."

I prayed a long time about whether to tell this next story of healing. My concern was—and is—that the story is not finished. Eventually I determined that it was meant to be included.

During the first five months of 1990, I made 22 trips bearing witness to the message of Medjugorje to as many people as possible. Included were tours of the Philippines, and Great Britain. I came home on the 18 of May, physically and mentally drained.

At the insistence of Terri, I was "on vacation" until sometime in July—no tours, no travel. It began a needed healing period of rehabilitation with wife and children; I went to little league baseball games, played some golf and sat through dance recitals—all the things that comprise normal, day-to-day family living.

A favorite little chore assigned to me by Terri, was to

pick up my six-year-old daughter Rebecca and two of her classmates from St Andrews School and drive them to dance classes. One of them was always the last to get ready: Courtney.

Courtney was a beautiful blond, blue-eyed waif who wasn't always in the best of health. The last to arrive, she would climb into the van and give me a big hug and say she was sorry to be late. I melted each time she did this, and I came to look on this child as one of my own.

So it was with shock that we received the news on Sunday morning, June 3rd: Courtney had collapsed at home and had been rushed to the emergency room of the local hospital. Just a few days before, she had attended Rebecca's sixth birthday party and was noticeably not acting well at that time. The diagnosis in the emergency room was devastating: Courtney had an inoperable tumor at the base of her brain. She had to be immediately flown by helicopter to the intensive care unit at Duke University Medical Hospital in Durham, North Carolina. Due to the urgency of getting her there without delay, her parents had to make the four-hour drive by automobile.

Kathian, Courtney's mother, called Terri. "Tell Wayne to please pray for Courtney!" she pleaded, after relating to Terri what had happened. They had only recently moved to Myrtle Beach, from California, and didn't know too many people. But she had read my book and knew of my involvement with Medjugorje.

After telling me about Courtney, Terri paused a moment and then asked, "What are we going to do?"

Neither of us knew why she asked the question in that way; she knew I would pray unceasingly and with aching heart for my little friend. But we were both surprised at my answer: "We need to go to the hospital so that I can pray over her."

We phoned Kathian the next day to ask if it was okay

for us to come. Within an hour, we had arranged for friends to take our children overnight, and were on our way.

During that long, four-hour drive, I prayed with intensity—and doubt. It was not doubt in the power of prayer, but in the one being asked to pray for this little girl. It was the enormity of the disease that created the lack of confidence and trust. At one point I was praying to Mary, that since I'd committed my life to doing things like this for her, maybe she could work a little harder on this one?

It was late at night by the time we arrived and had checked into a nearby motel. The elevator doors opened to the floor where the children's intensive care unit was located, and as we turned the corner, there were the anxious parents. We were soon brought up to date: Courtney was in a deep coma and her chances of survival were slim. Two of the most renowned specialists in the world had left the distraught parents with the statement that there was simply nothing more that they could do.

Kathian then quickly ushered me into the ward. My heart leaped and filled with apprehension when I saw the number of young children there—all special emergency cases. And there was Courtney, lying so still with all kinds of tubes running from her little body.

Trembling and unsure of myself, I took from my pocket a rosary that had been blessed in Medjugorje. "Kathian, I know you're Methodist, but this rosary came from Medjugorje—"

"Oh, thank you, thank you! I'm a former Catholic and I know the rosary." She immediately wrapped it around Courtney's wrist.

I didn't really know Kathian or Joe—only to say hello to at school functions or activities in which our daughters were involved. For that reason, I was a bit hesitant to say a great deal about Medjugorje and Our Lady's messages of prayer and fasting. I just knew it would work and only hoped the parents would understand beyond reaching for anything that would help their daughter. I did know that Joe had only recently begun attending the Methodist Church, and I was pleased later to hear him talking about praying and depending on God for Courtney's getting well.

"Well, I also have this holy oil," I continued, "and I'd like to anoint her if it's okay with you."

"Yes, yes, please!" Kathian urged. "Anything you want!"

For the next three hours I prayed over Courtney; I prayed every prayer I could remember, and then prayed in pleading conversational prayer with Jesus asking Mary to intercede for us. Finally when it was time to go, I prayed a little prayer to St Therese of the Child Jesus, my favorite saint, and the one I looked on as Our Lady's "first lieutenant."

"St Therese, Little Flower of Jesus, please, show me flowers—any kind of flowers—as a sign that Courtney is going to make it through this!"

As I walked out of the ward with Joe, I suddenly noticed on the large glass windows across from the elevator doors, huge posters of colorings of flowers, obviously done by small children and displayed on the children's wing.

I laughed in relief and thanksgiving, grabbing Courtney's father by the arm. "Joe, she's going to make it through this! I know it—I just know it!" And I did know it; that sign had never failed me.

Joe and I returned to the motel to get some sleep since I had to drive back home in a few hours, and he was totally exhausted. Terri stayed on the remainder of the early morning hours, talking with Kathian and praying for Courtney. When we left, Courtney's condition had not changed; she was still in a coma.

That evening I asked Terri to call Kathian at the hospital to find out what was happening. When she got through to her, Kathian excitedly exclaimed, "Courtney is awake! She awoke and began crying and asking for her daddy!" We all let out a shout and jumped for joy.

Silently I prayed a thank-you prayer to the Blessed Mother for asking Her Son to spare this child—and to St Therese for her beautiful sign. But then, Kathian gave us an even more beautiful sign.

"Terri," she began once we had all calmed down. "I was getting ready to call you! I have to tell you this: my best friend back in California called awhile ago to tell me about a strange dream she had."

Kathian paused to control her emotions before continuing. "My friend is a Lutheran, and of course, she doesn't know about Medjugorje, or about Wayne, or what he does. And you know, she doesn't know a whole lot about the Virgin Mary. Terri—she told me she had a strange dream last night that the Blessed Virgin Mary was holding Courtney in her arms, and there was a man standing next to her with his hand on Courtney—praying!"

When Terri related the story, I wept tears of joy.

How wonderful it would be to end this story right here. But as I related in the beginning, it isn't finished. Courtney has struggled with treatment, suffering from the pain and anguish of the after-effects and the medical treatments of radiation and chemotherapy. She is still a very sick little girl, and the outlook for her is not good. Yet she has continued to attend school when possible. Her parents have had to adjust to a new and difficult way of life in taking care of her.

I pray for her every day, sometimes every hour. And I see results: there has been great healing *around* Courtney—great healing from this little girl's *redemptive suffering* for others. She is a sign of hope and a symbol of love and faith for the children who attend St Andrews School, for her family, and for me. For the hundreds of people who have been touched by her, she has turned her cross into a cross of joy.

At Capernaum there happened to be a royal official whose son was ill. When he heard that Jesus had come back from Judea to Galilee, he went to him and begged him to come down and restore health to his son, who was near death. Jesus replied, "Unless you people see signs and wonders, you do not believe." "Sir," the royal official pleaded with him, "come down before my child dies." Jesus told him, "Return home. Your son will live." The man put his trust in the word Jesus spoke to him, and started for home. He was on his way there when his servants met him with the news that his boy was going to live. [John 4:46-51]

14

A Letter to Mary Virgin

"*Dear children, I have been inviting you for years by these messages which I am giving you. Little children, by means of the messages I wish to make a very beautiful mosaic in your heart so I may be able to present each one of you to God like the original image. Therefore, little children, I desire that your decisions be free before God, because He has given you freedom. Therefore, pray so that free from any influence of Satan, you may decide only for God. I am praying for you before God and I am seeking your surrender to God. Thank you for responding to my call.*" —*November 25, 1989*

Numerous times people have asked me, after a talk on the messages of Medjugorje, why I didn't say more about the Blessed Virgin Mary. My answer is simple: emotionally, I am not able to do it.

I love The Blessed Virgin with such intensity that the minute I begin speaking about her, I come unraveled. Besides, she desires that I concentrate on her Son, Jesus, just as she does.

That is the reason I love her so much: she is the one who led me to Jesus. It is this mother of the Living Word who has taught me to see Jesus as a real flesh-and-blood

Man-God, given in sacrifice for all our sins.

But writing about her is different. No one sees the tears or hears the quaver in the voice then; it allows me to say far more than I could standing before an audience. Also, I have time to think about what I want to say— something I've learned from receiving so many letters over the last five years. So, I felt that might be the best way for me to talk to you about her.

Dear Mary Virgin,

I wanted to write and thank you for all you have done in the last ten years through Medjugorje. My life will never be the same, especially after being touched by your personal invitation to be part of it all.

You came to this remote little village in the mountains of Yugoslavia, and you chose six children as conduits for thousands of messages you would deliver from your Son. And you continue to come. I personally think this is a miracle of the first magnitude—the most important one since the Resurrection of your Son, Jesus.

Mary, we hope and pray that your visits will continue. We still need you to teach us wisdom and love; we need you to continue to lead us out of the darkness of a world in utter turmoil and despair. The best part is, it's working! Millions are turning back to God!

We pray also, Mary, that the churches that claim to love God will pay attention and begin to heed your call and see that it is the same call issued by Jesus nearly 2,000 years ago. We pray that one day soon, we will attempt to fully live those wonderful words of Scripture and again be one church, one faith, one people under God, as it was in ancient days.

I think I know why God chose you for this seemingly impossible task, Mary. You are a mother; not a deity, not one who overshadows her Son, as so many like to think you do. They don't know you as we who have been touched by Medjugorje do. If they did, they would see a servant mother—a very human, loving, and caring servant mother.

You're certainly not a threat to anyone, except Satan. Your messages are not thundering prophecies of gloom and doom delivered by some ancient prophet. No, in fact, you're known as a gentle woman who comes to tell us to do what He tells us to do. And you've come throughout the ages to do the same thing when there was crisis in the world; places like Fatima, Lourdes and Guadeloupe. Besides, few ever listened to all the prophets; so why not send the Mother of the Living Word?

I believe He sent you, Mary, because you are a manifestation of the outpouring of the Holy Spirit. You are the handmaiden of the Father; you are the spouse of the Holy Spirit; and, you are the mother of the Son. We know that you come only under the power of the Holy Spirit, and your message is the presence of that Spirit.

Who can argue with what you've given us in these messages? You ask us to pray with the heart—unceasingly. That's what Jesus asked of us, and why He sent the Holy Spirit to us in His place. You request we fast on bread and water—just as Jesus did. And you tell us to do penance—love our neighbor, not just in words but in holy deeds of love. All of this leads to repentance and on-going conversion to God.

Can this but help our families return to being families again? Or teach us to be moderate in all things, as St. Paul admonishes? Is it not the only way we can save our youth today from the myriad of outside interests, pleasures and addictions that take them from us and from God?

Are we to be so hard-hearted and blind, as the Pharisees were in the days of Jesus' ministry, that through the wonderful gift of signs and miraculous healings, we cannot see the hand of God in these daily visits from you?

No, Mary. The fruit has been positive. My life has changed for the better, and so have the lives of millions of others touched by you at Medjugorje. I only pray that I will always be obedient to you and do just as your Son tells me to do. I only hope that I can imitate you in your love of the triune God.

Forgive me if this has been a little long, dear Mother of Jesus, but there's one more thing; we have these beautiful and elaborate shrines all over the world, and churches filled with relics and priceless art. We're awed by the splendor of such monuments to God. We live in high technology with superb communications equipment; and we have wonderful cities with millions of people in them. Any of these places or tools could have been used by you to come to us.

Yet, you chose a little village, with goats, sheep, chickens and pigs running loose; a place that is rocky and covered with bramble bushes and hard to reach; a spot now marked with a simple cross made by hammering two rough-hewn pieces of wood together.

It is here in this Bethlehem-like village, in this manger scene that you come to renew the Gospel message of Jesus Christ. It's as if you have given birth anew to the Savior of the World. You have poured out on us your grace.

Thank you, Mary Virgin. Thank you for coming and continuing to come. Thank you for allowing me to be a part of all this.

I love you, Mary.

Your son,
Wayne

"I, Mary Virgin, servant of God, very humble mother of Jesus Christ, Son of God, the Almighty and Eternal, to all who are in Messina, health and benediction in our Lord. You have learned by the ambassadors who have been sent to you. You received

the Gospel, and you acknowledged that the Son of God has become man and has suffered the passion and death for the salvation of the world, and that He is Christ, and also the true Messiah. I beseech you to persevere, promising to you, and all your posterity, to assist you in the presence of my Son."—by the Blessed Virgin Mary to the City of Messina where St. Paul preached the Gospel.

May the peace, the grace and the love of Jesus be with each of you.

Printed by Paraclete Press
Orleans, MA 02653
(800) 451-5006